How to Overcome Mental Tension

Swami Gokulananda

Ramakrishna Mission Institute of Culture

Gol Park, Kolkata - 700 029

E-mail : rmic@vsnl.com   Website : www.sriramakrishna.org

Published by

Swami Prabhananda
Secretary
The Ramakrishna Mission Institute of Culture
Gol Park, Kolkata-700 029, India

First Edition : July 1997 : 2,000
Twelfth Print : September 2006 : 10,000
Total Impression : 74,500

ISBN 81-85843-88-0

Computer typeset at
The Ramakrishna Mission Institute of Culture

Photo-offset at
Trio Process
P-128, C.I.T. Road
Kolkata 700 014

Foreword

This is a monograph which tells you why you suffer from mental tension and what you have to do to cope with it. Swami Gokulananda, the author, is not a psychiatrist. He is a monk to whom people of all age-groups come and unburden their minds. Why? It is difficult to say why. One reason perhaps is that he is loving and lovable. Once you meet him, you want to meet him again and again. Soon you discover he is a person to whom you can confide all your secrets. You tell him about things weighing on your mind. He gives you some advice and the advice turns out to be very helpful.

But how come that without being a psychiatrist Swami Gokulananda is able to give such advice ? It is because he meets people of all classes and he knows what are the common problems of man today. He has observed how selfish and greedy man is today and how he will go to any length to satisfy his desires. Self-control is the only solution to such problems, but to attain self-control is not that easy. The only way to control the mind is to direct it to more interesting things. Why do people risk life climbing mountains ? They love it. They find it more pleasant than anything else. It is a question of tastes you develop. Change the mind from one thing to another. The things that create tensions do no attract you any longer.

Swami Gokulananda's approach to the problem of tension is positive. He tells you what to do and he tells you what you may love to do. It is like learning how to swim. At first, you are nervous, but once you overcome your nervousness, you enjoy swimming. Most of the steps Swami Gokulananda asks you to take are like that. Once you start, you go on doing what he asks you to do merely for the pleasure of it.

The book is readable and highly useful to everybody in the present age.

4 July, 1997   **Swami Lokeswarananda**

Preface

The genesis of this book lies in the repeated requests I get as Secretary of Ramakrishna Mission, New Delhi, for personal interviews by people who are bogged down by the problems of life. Most of them come to discuss their personal problems and almost all these problems are related to mental tension. Therefore, I decided to give a series of lectures which were taped and edited to take the shape, finally, of this book.

It has been rightly said that the present century is a century of stress. The only way to control stress is to control the mind. Unless we know how to train the mind, it is very difficult to lead a purposeful life.

In these lectures, I have approached the problem of stress and its control from two standpoints—the Eastern and the Western. I have referred to what our ancient yogis said about mental control and also what the modern Western psychologists are saying about it at present.

One thing that has become obvious from this discussion is the psychosomatic nature of nervous tension and stress which cause major health hazards. The various conflicting urges and desires within us clamour for fulfilment simultaneously. Often there is a tug of war between the desires of the flesh and the aspirations of the spirit. The spirit is willing but the flesh is weak, as a famous saying tells us. The result is acute tension.

Mental stress can also arise due to an erroneous understanding of religion. As Sri Ramakrishna said in his usual pragmatic way, instead of suppressing desires, we should turn them towards higher goals. In other words, we should recycle them. The emphasis should be on sublimation rather than repression.

Apart from religion most people also have a wrong understanding of life itself. Excessive ambition, intellectual rivalry, overwork, the dual inner tendencies—extrovert and introvert—vying with each other, are all detrimental to peace of mind. To regain faith in ourselves we have to first have a balanced perspective of the meaning of existence. Instead of regretting the past or worrying over the future, we should give all our attention to the present.

Our aim should be to develop our will-power by avoiding useless talk, purposeless work, futile controversies, fault-finding tendencies, back biting, lurid thoughts, and all such distractions which dissipate our vital mental energies. Good thoughts bring rewards while bad thoughts bring punishment.

We should learn to review our mental processes from time to time. Praying to God for will-power or *icchha shakti* is essential, rather than praying for the transitory material gains. Concentrating on this single idea to the exclusion of all others is a sure path to success in curing mental tension.

We must have a positive attitude even in the face of the worst adversity. It is good to remember that even depression has a therapeutic side—it leads us to greater achievement. Depression brings to the forefront of our mind guilt, fear and anger which have to be faced before we can attempt to learn to control them.

The secret of achieving tranquility is to cultivate the attitude of acceptance and surrender. These are not passive attitudes but come only through great effort of meditation, introspection and self-analysis. The best method to achieve them is by what Swami Vivekananda called the *samanvaya yoga* which is also depicted in the emblem of the Ramakrishna Order. In it the sun stands for *jnana* or knowledge: the ability to discriminate between what is right and what is wrong; the lotus stands for *bhakti* or devotion: total faith in God's design for our lives and our acceptance of this divine design whole-heartedly. The waves in the water stand for *karma* or action: the ability to work in a disinterested manner without any overt anxiety about the result of our actions. And finally, the coiled serpent symbolises *raja yoga* or the technique by which one can achieve psychic control. Practising this *samanvaya yoga* in our everyday life is a sure cure for mental disturbance of any variety.

Once we have overcome tension we reach a dimension of inner bliss as is expressed in the immortal verse of the poet Rabindranath Tagore:

Remain in bliss in this world
Fearless, pure in heart
Wake up in bliss every morning,
Carry out all your duties in bliss,

Remain in bliss in weal and woe,
    In criticism and insult,
Remain in bliss unaffected,
Remain in bliss pardoning everybody!

This volume is an effort to bring this kind of continuous existential bliss within the reach of all people. It is hoped that all the readers of this volume will benefit immensely by practising sincerely and regularly all that is suggested in the following pages.

My sincere and deep debt of gratitude goes to Revered Swami Lokeswaranandaji, Secretary, Ramakrishna Mission Institute of Culture, Calcutta, for his kind and precious Foreword to this book which, I am sure, will greatly enhance the value of this book, and also for bringing out this publication from the Institute of Culture.

Before I conclude, let me record my gratitude to Prof. M.Sivaramakrishna and Dr. Sumita Roy of the Osmania University, Hyderabad, and Devipriya Guha Biswas, E.V.N.Chari, Malay Chatterji and others for all the help they have given in making this book acquire the present shape.

Swami Gokulananda

Contents

Contents

Introduction

I

Before we can talk about the steps through which mental tension is to be overcome it is essential to know the nature of what we call 'mental tension' and the causes which induce it.

Let me begin with a story about a doctor and one of his patients. The patient used to lead a very hectic life; he was constantly busy as he wanted to do everything for and by himself. The result was predictable: one day he broke down due to tremendous mental tension. He approached a doctor and described his problem. He said: "I have to do an enormous amount of work. Every day I am compelled to bring home a briefcase full of papers because I do not find enough time to complete the work in office. Consequently I am suffering from different kinds of tension. You are a doctor, so you should come to my rescue."

The doctor enquired, "Well, you work from morning till evening. Why, then, do you have to carry the files to your house?"

The patient answered, "I have to because I feel that no one else can do the work as well as I can do it myself. If I cannot finish the day's work before I go to office the next morning, I have more tension. In order to free myself from this tension, I am forced to work late in the night. Nevertheless, I am faced with other kinds of tension. I request you to examine me thoroughly and prescribe some medicine."

The doctor did not need to examine the patient thoroughly. He took a careful look at the patient and said, "Well, you must have implicit faith in me since you have come to me for help. Please follow all I have to say. Will you do exactly what I ask you to?"

The patient replied, "Yes, of course, I will. If I am going to be free from mental tension, I will do whatever you ask of me. In fact, I am eagerly waiting for your prescription."

The doctor said that he was not going to write out any medicines. "I shall only tell you orally. The prescription is that you should take off at least two hours every day from your hectic schedule and go for long walks. You should also take half a day's leave every week and spend it in a graveyard."

The doctor's prescription puzzled the patient greatly. He said with astonishment, "I came to ask you for some medicine to get rid of my mental tension and instead of giving me any medicine you ask me to go for long walks. It will cut into some of my precious time; nevertheless I am willing to follow your advice. But I don't understand why you suggest that I should spend a few hours every week in a graveyard?"

The doctor then gave a very significant explanation. He said, "I want you to go to a cemetery and look at the grave-stones of people who are there permanently because by doing so you will realise that death is a reality. You will meditate on the supreme fact of death; you will come to accept that the people buried there were like you before they died. They worked hard every day, all through their lives, thinking that the entire world rests on their shoulders. They too thought they were indispensable. When you die you will also be buried among them and others who take a walk in the cemetery will see your grave-stone and have similar thoughts. Realise the fact that even if a person who is leading a very hectic life dies, the world goes on as before in spite of his absence."

HOW TO OVERCOME MENTAL TENSION

This patient, unlike many others suffering from stress, at least had the patience to listen to the advice and he followed it, too. From then on, he tried to delegate his authority, stopped fretting and fuming and was able to get rid of his mental tension. For the rest of his life he led a balanced, integrated and peaceful life.

II

Like the "patient" I mentioned, most of us suffer from mental tension, fatigue and the stress and strain of life. In this connection what Swami Vivekananda says about the secret of work is extremely relevant. According to Swamiji, "The calmer we are, the less disturbed our nerves, the more shall we learn, the better will our work be."

The remarkable insight that Swamiji conveys to us through these words is that unless we subject ourselves to some kind of discipline we are likely to shatter our mental equilibrium into pieces.

An example makes this clear. A few months back an elderly couple came to me with their only son. Their whole life was built around this boy who was now very well placed, had a well-paid job and a good house in Delhi. But as happens with many young men, he fell in love with a girl belonging to a different community from that of his own. The parents were liberal and did not object to the marriage.

Gradually it so happened that the new daughter-in-law could not get on with the mother-in-law, although she was not so averse to the father-in-law. Soon she prevailed upon her husband to take a separate house and they moved out. It was a tremendous shock to the parents; it caused them great mental tension and strain. The boy was their only son and with what great expectations they had brought him up! They came and requested me to suggest a solution to their problem. I said, "Can you bring the boy to me one day?"

"We shall try."

"Does your son come to see you?" I asked.

"Yes, my son comes occasionally but his wife does not come at all. For some reason she does not seem to like visiting us."

"All right. Bring him one day and let me have a talk with him."

After a fortnight I got a telephone call from the father saying that he would come with his son. I was very optimistic of settling the issue. At least I would have, I felt, an opportunity of talking to the son. But when he came I noticed that he too had his own quota of mental tension. I realised that he did not want to return to his parents and stay with them.

But soon he had a strained relationship with his wife. He had, naturally, further mental tension. He moved out of the house he occupied with his wife and went back to his parents. I was sure that now there would be some sort of reconciliation. Unfortunately, that was not to be. After offering him tea and snacks I listened to the son's story. He said that he had to return to his parents because his wife had deserted him.

I asked, "All right, what do you want to do now?"

"Even though she has deserted me," he said, "I cannot desert her. I want to regain her love. I want to be united with her."

Strange are the ways of God! This is a common enough phenomenon, especially in cities like Delhi. And it is not the only cause of tension.

Let me illustrate with another story. One day a family came to me. They were residing outside

India. They had only one daughter and after their return to Delhi they were finding it very difficult to get her admitted to a good school. This was the source of considerable anxiety and tension to them. Similarly, another couple came and told me they wanted their daughter to study in a good school but to admit her there, they themselves had to face an interview! Of course, this was the cause of much worry and stress.

Sometimes the devotee says, "Well, Swamiji, I want to lead a very relaxed life; but I also want to be efficient. Even if I work at a tremendous pace for eight hours at office, the work does not get completed. As a result I work faster and longer which causes great tension. And sooner or later, I find myself going to pieces over small things and that causes terrible irritation to me."

This is not a particular instance; it is the picture of more or less the whole world today. Everywhere we are now faced with the hustle and bustle of life, racing against time and ending up with tension and fatigue. Whatever may be our attitude towards life, we cannot just get away from the fact that nervous tension has become a regular phenomenon, as it were. It is no surprise then that we rarely find a person leading a quiet, normal and balanced life, a person who is calm and collected and can rise above any adverse circumstance.

The crucial question is: Do we work properly these days? Our ancestors did not lead hectic lives. They did work, but we do not work like them because we always seem to be in a rush. We do not even have time to eat properly. We somehow gulp down whatever we have to take at a break-neck speed, either while sitting in a revolving chair in the office or while watching television at home.

What is to be emphasised is that most of us are in a very highly strung frame of mind all the time. Suppose we are driving a car constantly at top gear, we are bound to have an accident. In our work we often go into high gear and inevitably suffer from severe mental tension. Thanks to the modern conditions of life created by science and technology, we have reduced ourselves to bundles of excitable and explosive nerves.

Is it not a fact that most of us living in this century are tense, tired, miserable and unhappy? We suffer from so much nervous tension and stress that writers characterise this century as the century of stress. We also believe that this is the normal state for human beings; for, in today's world if we have to live, we have to live with stress and strain. So goes the argument.

Of couse, some of us do want to take preventive measures for stress-induced maladies such as heart-attack, blood pressure; we dutifully go to a doctor periodically to have a routine medical check-up. In spite of the check-up, the fact is that we remain unhappy and tense. We can put up a calm exterior but our face, the index of our mind, shows our worry, our tension.

III

Now let us enumerate the reasons for this tension. The first and most basic reason is that we are drifting endlessly. Perceiving the truth of this statement may well be the key which unlocks the door to a meaningful life. People who realise this and lead a purposeful life are, of course, exceptions; they live happily. But others who suffer from mental tension cannot be said to be living at all. At the most we can say that they exist; they vegetate. There is a vast difference between leading a purposeful life and existing only like a vegetable. Mental tension causes such intense suffering that people prone to it can never be happy; their worst and deadliest enemy is constant stress. But there are people even in this century of stress who know that somehow they have to come to terms with the existence of stress and use it to their advantage.

Obviously, the question arises as to the method of taming stress and using it to our advantage. We shall take up this aspect of the issue a little later. At present it is sufficient to highlight the point that we have to resolve to lead a healthy, creative, motivated life in the century of stress; we can adopt certain means by which we rise above the circumstances that cause stress and strain. But if we fail in that resolve we shall be at the mercy of mental tension and the untold misery which it brings.

Let us illustrate this with the typical instance of a busy executive in a big business house. He is always busy and always suffering from mental tension. When he comes home he carries his tension home with him. He thinks, "All the time I am working in the office from nine in the morning to six or seven in the evening, I am tense. If I find a congenial atmosphere at home I shall get mental peace." But he does not find what he is looking for due to his own fault.

When he comes home and tells his wife, "Oh, I am under terrible strain. There was terrible tension in the office." She understands his plight immediately and stays away from him. She tells the children not to go near their father or disturb him because he is not in a good mood. The husband has carried his tension home.

Once a person suffers from tension, he communicates it to others. He is all the time unhappy and agitated. This produces an atmosphere of unrest and tension around him. No one comes near him. But if a person leads a balanced and calm life he conveys a sense of happiness to the others who come into contact with him.

There is another aspect of tension: a person who is suffering greatly from tension might become, say, a slave to anger. He will then fret and fume and his face will acquire a red hue, his eyes will become bloodshot, his eyebrows will be constantly drawn together in a frown. These

HOW TO OVERCOME MENTAL TENSION

internal chemical changes leave a pronounced impact on the face and expression of such a person. Many doctors corroborate that a person who is in a fit of anger can have a stroke as his heart-beat goes up from 180 to 200 per minute. Usually we are not aware of such dire consequences. Similar is the case with certain physical ailments such as headache, backache, high blood pressure, indigestion, fatigue, which are all due to emotional stress.

All this happens or we allow it to happen because we are ourselves drifting in a sort of neutral mental gear. As I have mentioned in the beginning, if we go in high gear, we are sure to meet with accidents whereas we make no progress if we are in neutral gear.

What does this neutral mental gear mean? It means that we are not conscious of the great power that is lying hidden within us. As Swami Vivekananda said repeatedly, "Man is not just a lump of flesh. Man is omnipotent, divine, the infinite spirit." He also said that once we are conscious of our innate divine nature and can manifest it, then power, strength, purity and all that is excellent comes to us. But if we are not conscious of the great power which is at the back of our limited physical frame we shall naturally continue to be in a sort of neutral mental gear.

But once we are aware that there is something divine in us we can change the situation. A person may say, "I often become a victim of different kinds of emotional stress including anger and I realise later that I did not behave properly." Every person who loses his temper may regret the angry words he uttered by saying, "I should not have behaved in that way. I was not master of myself. I lost control over myself and that is why I behaved so badly. Please forgive me."

This is a part of our everyday experience. But once we become aware of the divinity in us and the potential for infinite strength we can no longer continue to live in a sort of neutral mental gear. We realise the supreme truth of the divine spark within us. As our great rishis have said, we have infinite power to feel free and that infinite power is within us. So long we have lived in darkness and depression without realising that there is a thought-switch in us. All that we have to do is to turn it on and get the light of happiness. Therefore now is the time

that we should be aware of this, now itself!
There is something divine in us and if we can
connect ourselves to that current which is the
source of infinite strength, we will be able to
lead a happy life, in a natural way.

IV

Since mental tension is the result of our
activities, let us analyse our daily routine. Our
day-to-day activity can be divided into four
different life areas. We have our work: we go to
our field of work. Then we come home to our
family and children; this is another aspect of our
life. Sometimes we go out, get an invitation from
a friend to go for a picnic, a birthday party or
some other special occasion. This is our social
commitment. Thus, society and friends
constitute another area of life. In addition, one
has moments of leisure such as sports, going to
the club, watching television, which is the last
of the four areas of life.

Mental tension may differ in each life area.
For example, some may face an excessive
nervous tension during work, but very little at
home due to an understanding wife. Suppose
something happens in the office, as for instance,

the boss is cross with his subordinate and gives him work which he does not like. Since he has to earn his livelihood, the subordinate is helpless; he cannot refuse to do the unpleasant work. He has to make adjustments and this causes acute mental tension. He comes back home. If he finds a sweet, loving, understanding wife who can share the agonies of her husband, there is peace. Otherwise the situation becomes unbearable.

Similarly, suppose a person is working in a particular field and suddenly his field of work is changed. He is given some responsiblity in another field and his superior tells him, "From now on you have to handle this new responsibility," but he finds the work boring; it is not challenging enough for him. He naturally loses all interest in his work. This may give rise to nervous tension. This is because he is bored, has no challenges to overcome and finds himself drifting. But in such a situation we should be able to make adjustments.

In any case, as we noted already, we should be aware of the fact that tension/stress is part of life today. We should be able to use it to our advantage rather than be defeated by it. We have to, as it were, recycle it so that we have a healthy, well-balanced and integrated life. For this the right kind of motivation is needed since right motivation is an antidote to tension and stress. A person without right motivation is like a ship without a rudder.

In this connection a very important and relevant observation was made by Martin Luther King who had a very pragmatic approach to life's conflicting problems and challenging situations. He said, "The ultimate measure of a person is not where he stands in moments of comfort and convenience, but where he stands in times of challenge and controversy."

Mark the words "in moments of comfort and convenience." When there is no challenging situation, no adverse context, no bereavement, where husband and wife are not suffering from any tension, where children are all happy, where good alone results and nothing is wrong, we are sure to have peace. But the ultimate measure or worth of a person is not to be judged when he is living in a peaceful environment but when he is face to face with adversity. If he can keep his balance or mental equilibrium then such a person is to be given the highest marks. In moments of comfort and convenience we do not have nervous tension or stress. But when challenging situations stare us in the face, the way in which we respond physically and emotionally is the yardstick of our success in dealing with nervous tension. If we can rise to the occasion and meet the situation boldly, that is real success.

It so happened that when Swami Vivekananda went to Varanasi once he was chased by a group of monkeys near Durgabari. The natural reaction of an average person to such a situation would be fear. Swamiji too wanted to run away lest the monkeys do him harm. Just then a monk shouted to him, "Face the brutes." Swamiji turned back and faced the monkeys. Immediately they ran away. Thus, challenging situations do come as life cannot be all sunshine. There are bound to be rainy days—adverse situations— but we have to meet every challenging situation boldly, being fully conscious of the fact that we have the power to overcome the situation. Therein lies our manliness. We should always remember this. This is the implication of those significant words by Martin Luther King.

xxx   HOW TO OVERCOME MENTAL TENSION

V

We should not, however, think that only those who work hard are subject to different kinds of mental tension. No one is free from it. But there are various approaches which lead to the solution of this problem. The orthodox approach is available in medical science which may be described as follows: suppose someone is suffering from stress, tension or fatigue or has a nervous breakdown and goes to a doctor. The medical doctor may fail to recognise the root of the problem. He may treat the symptoms while the patient remains without treatment. It must be remembered that the patient is not merely the body; he has a mind too. The doctor may not give importance to the patient's mental state and the effect it is having on the body. A person suffering from mental tension may complain of headache, backache, or hypertension. The doctor may treat him only physically. If the patient goes to a psychiatrist he has to spend a large amount of money. I had occasion to hear of parents who had to spend such huge sums of money for the treatment of their children. In such cases my advice is, "Forget all about that. Have faith in your inner divinity. Follow Swamiji, meditate on him and soon you will get rid of your malady." In some cases this has proved successful. It shows that what we need is a proper blending of the mind-body complex. Unlike the orthodox medical approach, the modern approach is that we look towards both the body and the mind of the patient.

Here let me mention a significant article by John R. Harvey called "An Overview of Stress and Stress Management." In it he has narrated his own experiences. I would like to recount one of them briefly. One day a friend of Harvey came to his office looking very anxious and related to him the medical history of his family. He said that his great-grandfather who was robust and enjoyed good health all his life had a heart attack at the age of 78; his grandfather, a self-made man who had his own business had a heart attack when he was 68; his father was only 58 years old when he had a fatal heart attack. He told Harvey with a sigh of resignation, "After all this I think I won't go beyond 48." After some moments of silence he recovered himself and asked, "Well, Mr.Harvey, why is this happening? Why are they dying progressively younger?" There was silence for some more time and once again the friend said, "Is there something I can do to prevent such a thing happening to me?"

Mr. Harvey writes in his article that after listening to his friend he gave the matter serious thought. He reflected deeply. The friend was in a crisis when he asked these questions exactly as many of us might be during some stage of our life. And John Harvey's suggestion to his friend is applicable to all of us. He told his friend, "Why do you think that you won't go beyond 48? Why do you indulge in negative thinking? Take up a positive attitude. Follow certain disciplines; go according to the mode of life I suggest and you will also live to be as old as your great-grandfather." The friend did as he was told and lived a long life.

Similar questions can be raised by many others. Today most people have financial security; they have material comforts and success. But they have to pay a price for this. Each achievement is accompanied by some kind of nervous tension, fatigue and ultimately fatal diseases leading to death. Nervous tension seems to be a major cause of death.

A significant point to note here is that stress can be controlled. Some time back the Government of India released a stamp with a three-word message—"Avoid Negative Stress." This can be interpreted to mean that if stress is properly motivated it can be tamed to do us good. Used negatively, it creates jealousy, hatred, suspicion, anger, nervous tension, fatigue and other maladies.

VI

From this it is evident that stress can be classified as positive and negative. Positive stress is to be welcomed as it gives us incentive to work and a desire to do it well. Otherwise we would be content with what we have and avoid adversity. We would refuse to meet challenges and humanity would then have continued to live in the stone age even today.

We constantly have some kind of stress. Let it be positive stress and not a negative one because negative stress engenders an unwelcome situation. It aggravates thoughts which are full of unhappiness and distress.

Let me illustrate negative stress by an example. Suppose there are two colleagues who would like to supercede each other. In course of time one is placed above the other. The situation is naturally very painful and the resultant nervous tension is inevitable, quite often intolerable. But this kind of situation has to be handled in such a way that it becomes a spur to more concentrated effort.

There is a mistaken notion that if we work for long hours—fifteen or sixteen per day— we suffer from tension. But there are instances to show that people have worked for about twenty hours without complaining of any ill effects provided the work environment is favourable and the company congenial. In cases where the environment is hostile even a few hours of work will seem stressful. From this we can conclude that fatigue relating to work is more a state of the mind rather than of the body.

Chapter 1

Stress and the Body-mind Complex

In modern society there are different kinds of diseases and nervous tension can also be counted as one of them. But it is different from most other diseases because there is no germ or virus causing it. It is the result of the malfunctioning of the body-mind interaction. In other words, we can say that nervous tension is a psychosomatic disease in the true sense of the term. The word "psyche" means the mind and "soma" means the body. Nervous tension is the result of the way we have consciously or unconsciously chosen to live. When we speak of tension we should understand that the primary need of the mind and the body is that the mental and physical functioning be regulated.

Nervous tension is a kind of recurring imbalance resulting in the daily wear and tear of the body. The two aspects of it which we need to understand are how it occurs and how we give expression to it. It comes in different guises, so to say. It may take the form of emotional or mental stress which is generated by our personality as it interacts with the environment every day. This can also be called "social stress." In addition, there is another form of stress called the "digestive stress." It is the tension which results due to our poor eating habits. Therefore, it would be a mistake to think that the causes of stress are merely external: at home or in the place of work, that overwork alone causes stress. There are many other causes, such as poor eating habits, for example.

Apart from these we have another common form of stress called environmental stress in the present times. It may be the result of many factors such as smog, noise and air pollution.

Each of us thus has a psychophysical system in the body which reflects our state of mind through physical diseases. If we suffer from nervous tension, fatigue or tremendous strain at the mental level, it is sure to come out in the form of aches and pains or more serious diseases such as hypertension, ulcer, stroke, cancer, heart attack and others. In fact, the doctors and psychologists are strongly of the opinion that most diseases are closely linked with a state of sustained nervous tension which has become an invariable component of our daily routine.

Sustained nervous tension is therefore a common phenomenon today. It stems directly from different kinds of frustration, worry and despondency. Each day we have to meet various forms of challenges at home, in our place of work or even at play. These are in addition to the ordinary demands imposed on our mind and body by the process of living. The result of this is acute nervous tension which shows itself in the form of impatience, anger, anxiety or fear. If we take an unhealthy diet, or if we have the habit of smoking, drinking or an addiction to drugs, they too result in different kinds of tension. In short, we can say that we are living in a world of tensions.

Even in the course of our routine work we sometimes experience tension. Travelling by public transport or buying the necessities of daily life may also produce mental stress. For instance, we are on our way to the airport to catch a particular flight. On the way the taxi or scooter is held up due to traffic congestion or such other factors. This is bound to cause considerable mental tension.

Technological advances, industrialisation, and excessive urbanisation have given rise to situations which produce dangerous emotional strains. That is why diseases such as asthma and hypertension have become so rampant. Also, people who suffer from such diseases take to drinking or consuming dangerous drugs in desperation. But their addictions cannot give them permanent relief. The temporary relief which they get has its own repercussions: they cause further and more serious problems which lead not only to psychosomatic but also psychiatric illnesses, in some extreme cases to suicide also.

The need is to search for a viable solution. In talking about nervous tension we should never be pessimistic. By being optimistic we can begin to look for the ideal situation. The first step to this will be when we wake up in the morning and feel fresh as a daisy. We have sufficient energy. For this it is essential that we sleep well. If we have deep, undisturbed sleep we can work hard the whole day without undue haste, agitation or unnecessary excitement. We can work for long hours calmly and methodically. In the evening we come back home with a feeling of natural tiredness. But this is not a problem because it can be cured by a good night's sleep.

But such is not the case with everybody. In a majority of cases the natural fatigue is superseded by unbearable stress and tension. People are in the grip of constant tension because they have not mastered the way of working in a calm and methodical manner. We all work but we do not know how to relax. We continue to work in such a way that the tension increases. With the passage of time it becomes progressively more difficult to get real peace of mind. As a result we become worn out, exhausted, so to say and often feel oppressed and irritable.

The daily routine of such people becomes disagreeable as they have to put in much effort to do habitual jobs. Work becomes a drudgery. It is such people who often suffer from tremendous mental strain, fatigue and bewildering change of moods. Sometimes they become the victims of morbid ideas, subject to dejection, depression and despondency. Whatever little energy they have is exhausted in this manner and they are reduced to inert objects. Their will-power also reaches the lowest ebb. They are unable to decide what has to be done the next day.

The work which such people do the whole day is haphazard and unsystematic. The tremendous pressure under which they work does not allow them to do the job with the right spirit. They consider their tasks as drudgery and each day seems an unending torture. The only outcome of this attitude is an increase in mental tension. They become oversensitive and cannot even bear any sudden little sound. They are irritated, for instance, by the ringing of the telephone, the banging of a door or the barking of a stray dog. They over react in all such situations.

The first step to overcome such acute mental tension is to understand the nature of stress and also to learn about the workings of the human mind. The anatomy and psychology of mental tension must be known clearly before it can be alleviated.

Let me illustrate this: Suppose a person is

working in Delhi. He lives there happily with his family when his boss suddenly transfers him to Bombay or any other city. He has to go there. The problem is that he has an establishment here and he has to set up another in the new place. He is helpless and has to go. He worries about the admission of the children. He tries everywhere but does not manage to put the children in good schools. Since he is not a Government employee, his children do not get admission in a Central School and this creates further tension. He stays in Bombay for some time, say for a month, all the time undergoing acute mental agony. As a result he falls a victim to some serious disease.

Then there is the case of a demanding wife telling her husband that he has achieved nothing in life. Once I went to such a house where the husband was the only son in the family. He was a very brilliant student. His wife told me, "Maharaj, I am not happy. My husband was in England. He had many friends there. They have all come up in life. But my husband has done nothing to come up like them. We don't even have a car or a good house." She was complaining like this. To help her, I invited the couple to the Ashrama but the wife did not come more than once or twice though the husband came many times. She was suffering from tremendous depression. The husband is well-placed, a brilliant student of the Calcutta University and has a senior gazetted post at present. But to his wife all this seemed inadequate.

As against this illustration, let us now cite an example of an understanding wife. In 1992 when I was in Frankfurt I was the guest of a family of devotees staying there. They looked after me very well and took me in their car from Frankfurt to Geneva. They were very good people, a happy family with two nice daughters. After my return to India, I learnt that the husband lost his job. I was terribly shocked. Fortunately the wife was working and in those places there is some provision to give an allowance to people who have no employment. The wife struggled to make both ends meet. She gave all the support to her husband by saying, "Don't lose heart, my beloved husband. Better days will come. I am with you. I am earning and I shall be able to support the family." Some time later I got a telephone call from the wife and she told me that her husband had found a good job. I was overwhelmed with emotion. The husband could obviously sustain the tremendous strain because of an understanding wife. What a contrast to the wife who makes her husband's life miserable!

There are also cases of a demanding husband. Let me describe a typical case in Delhi. Here both the husband and the wife were working in good positions. The wife soon began to earn more because of her sincerity and hard work. The husband became jealous. He wondered, "Why does my wife get more salary and why do I get less?" He was suffering from an inferiority complex. Due to this he began making unreasonable demands on the wife. If she came a little late he demanded angrily, "Why are you late?" He often telephoned her office which caused awkwardness and embarrassment. He was not at all understanding. As soon as she returned from office he would order her, "You must cook food for me at once." Suppose the next morning the wife has to leave early to office the husband who had an inferiority complex said, "Why are you going early? You have to iron my clothes." Such things are unpleasant but inescapable facts in some families.

On the other hand there is the case of the understanding husband. I would like to give you a complete picture and not a one-sided picture. Therefore it is essential to give this illustration. If both the husband and the wife have jobs and help each other in the daily chores it is ideal. If the husband comes from office and finds his wife tired he does not mind taking over all the work in the kitchen, telling his wife, "You take rest, you are tired. I am here to look after the children. I shall also cook for you and the other members of the family." In such a case there are no tensions and misunderstandings in the house.

Another aspect which has to be considered seriously is the impact of parental tensions on children. If there is no understanding between husband and wife in a family it has an adverse effect on the children. Parents have to be extra careful so that they do not subject their children to the trauma of sharing the increasing agitation and worries of their parents. The present world is difficult for children in the normal course of things: they have to work very hard at school, they breathe polluted air, and when they come back home they find a congenial atmosphere lacking there. The parents quarrel all the time and this tells upon the nerves of the children.

I have quoted these instances to show you the kinds of people who are susceptible to nervous tension. But the aim is not to be pessimistic and give way to depression. What we have seen till now is the darker side of stress but there is also the other side of the coin: nervous tension can bring some benefits and advantages. It is up to us to know how to use nervous tension to our best advantage.

Today people all over the world are anxious about the problem of mental tension; scholars, psychologists, psychotherapists, are all disturbed by the situation. Doctors and psychiatrists have been trying to determine the causes of tension and conflicts and search out remedies by which to overcome the problem.

Let us catalogue the different causes of tension by considering a series of cases. For instance, if the head of a family leads a balanced life and is never agitated, it is sure to have a salutary effect on all the members of the family. But if he leads an agitated life, always fretting and fuming, angry and aggressive, there will be no peace in the family. The first thing to note is that tension is present in certain individuals. Next, this tension percolates in inter-personal relationships.

Tension in a group or community is the next in line of this spreading chain of stress. Suppose we live in an apartment which has three floors. The tenant is on the top floor, someone else on the first floor and the landlord on the ground floor. All may be on good terms till tension is generated around some particular problem. For instance, one of them has an Alsatian dog which barks loudly and keeps the others awake. The others object and the owner of the dog gets angry at the criticism of his beloved dog. This leads to unpleasantness and there is tension in social relationships.

The basic necessity for the removal of nervous tension completely from our mind is to have a clear understanding of the causes of tension. For this, in turn, we must know the workings of the human mind. Nervous tension is no doubt psychosomatic but it depends mainly on the mind. If the mind is healthy, we can get rid of nervous tension.

Frankly speaking, nervous tension is not restricted to householders alone. Even some monks and brahmacharins suffer from it. Sometimes they cannot acclimatise themselves to the schedule; they just leave and go to the Himalayas. When they return, if they are asked why they left so suddenly, they reply that they had been suffering from some kind of mental fatigue. This is a fairly common phenomenon.

I remember an incident. Once a brahmachari approached a senior monk and said, "Maharaj, I am under terrible mental depression." Fortunately, the monk was an out and out Sankarite, a staunch Advaitavadin. He looked at the young brahmachari and said, "Oh, you are suffering from mental depression! I see! Now tell me, are you the mind, or the body or the Eternal Spirit?"

The young brahmachari got his answer, a solution to his problem of stress. He said, "When I do not forget my divine heritage and the higher dimensions of my life, I am the Atman; then I am neither the body, nor the mind, nor the sense organs and there is no problem. But when I forget my true nature and come down to the lower plane and identify myself with the body, mind, or the desires of the mind, its feelings and other sensations associated with the body, I suffer."

In effect, the answer given by the senior monk to the brahmachari is applicable to all who are prone to mental tension or depression: as long as we have fragmentary perception and associate reality with the body/mind we suffer. Why do we associate reality with the unreal mind? If you believe that Atman alone is real and you are that Atman, then you have no problem. Fortunately, the brahmachari understood this immediately. He came back from his meeting with the senior monk fully satisfied. He realised that his mistake was in putting limitations to overshadow his real self with unreality. The cure to his problem, and to that of all who have a similar problem is to be conscious of our real nature.

If we have to find remedies for nervous tension, we must be aware of the workings of the human mind. According to Hindu psychologists, such as Patanjali, there are five states of mind. Sometimes the mind is called *kshipta* (extremely restless) when it is prone to tension, emotional conflicts and worries. It can also be *mura* (inert); we often find people who are dull and inert under the influence of tension. Each of these states of the mind is under the influence of one of the three gunas. In the *kshipta* state the mind is under the influence of *rajas*, which is characterised by constant activity full of tension. The *mura* state is one of *tamas* where the mind is prone to passions such as *kama*, *krodha*, and so on and so forth. Patanjali spoke of a third state, that is *vikshipta*, a state in which the mind is at times able to attain partial concentration. It is possible to have a state which is in between these.

Let me illustrate this with an example. Suppose a son is disobedient. If he is under the influence of *kshipta* and you try to control him, he will revolt; in the state of *mura* he will not react; in the state of *vikshipta* he may or may not listen to you. In moments of sanity he may admit that your words have truth and he is willing to obey you; at other times he may do as he wishes.

The fourth of the states identified by Patanjali is *ekagrata* (concentrated state). This can be seen in people deeply absorbed in their work: for instance, a person absorbed in study, a painter painting or a singer singing, or a person working in the office with total dedication, in the true spirit of a karma yogi. All these people display the mind full of concentration of the *ekagra chitta*. The last of the five states is called the *niruddha* state. It is a superconscious state which is akin to samadhi and not many people can attain to it.

To summarise the five states once more so that they leave an indelible impression on our minds, let me repeat Patanjali's categorisation: (1) *Kshipta* (extreme restlessness); (2) *Mura* (inert); (3) *vikshipta* (partly concentrated); (4) *ekagrata* (fully concentrated); and (5) *niruddha* (superconscious).

To illustrate the last two states I will give the example of meditation in a temple. Sometimes when you come to the temple and sit down to meditate you may become absolutely immersed and not wish to leave your seat for a long time. As a bhakta if you concentrate on your Ishta Devata you may be so deeply merged in the deity that you are absolutely unconscious of your surroundings. You are enjoying spiritual bliss from within; such a situation is possible when the mind is in the *niruddha* and *ekagrata* states.

Swami Vivekananda, as a great yogi, had experience of these states. In his famous lecture on Raja Yoga he dealt with the second yoga aphorism of Patanjali. In his explanation he referred to the five states of the mind and said, "The *chitta* or mind manifests itself in the following forms: scattering, darkening, gathering, one-pointed and concentrated."

To elaborate this: by scattering Swamiji meant the *kshipta* state in which most of us fritter away valuable energies. As a cure to this Sri Aurobindo, the great saint of Pondicherry, taught that we must learn the technique of training the mind in such a way that we can gather our energies for some useful purpose. He said, " We must know how to gather ourselves up." Instead of doing this most of us are just dissipating our energies in different directions which results in suffering. Concentration of the mind or *ekagra chitta* is the sine qua non of a really peaceful and integrated life and to arrive at 'this state we have to know how to gather ourselves up. That is what Swamiji also meant when he spoke about people who are unable to find solace as they are scattering their valuable energies.

The next description given by Swamiji is darkening, that is, *mura* which does not react in either a good or a bad manner. Under the influence of tension it is inert like a stone. The act of gathering is to collect the energies and focus our attention on our divine self, because that is our true nature. This is difficult as we use up the valuable mental resources in the pursuit of phantom pleasures of the world and the precious human birth goes in vain. The mind is diverted from the true self and its divine nature. So the mind which is *kshipta* or *mura* should be brought under control by the act of gathering or *vikshipta*. Though the mind is prone to move in different directions, an aspirant and a seeker of truth has to make an effort to gather it together.

This state of concentration is followed by *ekagrata* or one-pointedness. For instance, in this state a person who sits for meditation is successful. The mind is still and does not wander aimlessly. In the lotus or temple of the heart such a person visualises the picture of his beloved deity, a living smiling presence, effulgent and compassionate, showering blessings. It is an experience of unending joy in the company of the chosen ideal. This is possible only in the state of *ekagrata*. If a person can remain in this state for long he is preparing the way for the next state, that is, *niruddha*. In such a state, as Swamiji said, "There is no more birth and death and I become free."

These five states of mind—*kshipta, mura, vikshipta, ekagrata* and *niruddha*, according to Patanjali—and scattering, darkening, gathering, one-pointed and concentrated according to Swamiji are to be remembered carefully before we can talk about solving the problem of stress. Every day we should make a sort of self-analysis—"Before I begin my day's work I should try to analyse whether I am in the state of *kshipta* or *mura*. If the former state prevails I shall not be successful in whatever I do and this will result in tension. If I am in the *vikshipta* state I shall succeed but this is not the end. I shall have to aim at being *ekagra chitta*. This will bring me to a tension-free state."

In this way awareness of the workings of our own mind and its impact on bodily responses goes a long way in overcoming mental tension.

Chapter 2

Role of Higher Values in Resolving Mental Tension

In view of what has been said so far we can identify one of the major causes of mental tension as the presence of different urges in us. For example, as far as religious ideals are concerned we have our basic, primary urges. In addition we have many desires of the body and the mind, biological urges, primitive urges and such others. Tension may be caused even by the presence of some of the higher values in life. A person who is religiously inclined and wants to proceed towards the perfection of higher life and experience, spiritual bliss is held back by certain physical limitations. This could create tension.

This idea is clearly enunciated in the Katha Upanishad where the God of Death tells Nachiketa that human beings have been created in such a way that they cannot but want to enjoy the outside world. Only in rare moments of inner awareness we are conscious of a divine spark in us. Even then our biological urges pull us down towards the mundane things of the physical plane. This results in a situation where a person is aware of the presence of perfection within and is eager to reach it but is hindered by powerful urges. Obviously, the result of this conflicting pull is tension. Thus, the divine urge on one side and the biological urge on the other are engaged in a tug of war which causes no small tension.

In this connection we would do well to recall to mind a person who did pioneering work in the field of psychotherapy in the West and whom students of psychology know intimately through his work—Sigmund Freud. According to Freud, it is the biological urges that create conflict in the mind. Although in the beginning Freud called this primitive biological urge as the sex urge, later he modified the language and termed it the "pleasure principle." This is indicative of the fact that there is an urge in each of us through which we derive the maximum amount of pleasure in this very life.

In the context of such pleasure I am also reminded of what the Carvak Philosophy tells us. According to it we have to follow the maxim of "eat, drink and be merry"––that is, the hedonistic ideal. The existence of God, soul, and such matters are negated. The main thrust of their teaching is that since you have this human birth it is better to enjoy physical pleasure, sense pleasure, as much as possible. But in a person who has some consciousness of higher values this urge to get intense physical pleasure does not find a chance for proper expression and the resulting conflict is extremely stressful. Rarely are there people who can sublimate their desire for sense pleasures. Of course, that is a point we shall take up elsewhere. At present our main concern is to consider the basic physical urges in ordinary human beings.

Apart from the hindrance of higher values in the path of acquiring physical pleasure, there is, in terms of Freudians, the element called superego. This superego also provides effective censorship to the urge for pleasure and the mind prevents the body from finding an outlet for this.

At this point it could be better to admit candidly that human beings are subject to powerful physical desire which they want to fulfil at all costs. For instance, a young, college-going boy or girl is enjoying a lurid film on cable TV when the parents come home. They do not approve of their son/daughter seeing such a film. They are deeply religious. The son/daughter gets frightened because he/she is aware of this censorship and stops seeing the film though he/she wants to see it very desperately.

It is also possible that the boy/girl places restrictions on himself/herself in the fulfilment of pleasure. If a young person has developed certain higher values in life, or has been initiated into spiritual disciplines, he/she does not think it right to enjoy such cheap films because of the realisation that such things bring him/her down. But left alone he/she often gives in to the urge for the expression of pleasure even while knowing that it should be avoided. This causes untold misery due to conflict and tension.

The spiritual urge, thus, has its own contribution to the enhancement of stress. The scriptures say, "Don't do this, don't do that." Their injunctions impel us to attain purity in thought, word and deed. When we go against these in spite of professing a belief in them there is sure to be chaos. This awareness is the superego which acts as a censor on the urges of the mind and prevents the expression of the pleasure principle. And, when this principle does not find proper expression it is repressed or suppressed: it remains dormant in the unconscious regions of our mind, creating further tension.

Therefore it has been said that religious ideals prevent one from pursuing the path of pleasure. A person who is haunted by an intangible sense of guilt cannot fulfill his desire for pleasure. His conscience troubles him and causes a conflict. Then there is the fear of criticism from people around which also causes mental tension. All this adds up to the fact that people who are not much concerned with higher values can devote their time to the pursuit of pleasure.

Another cause of mental tension is the erroneous understanding of religion which is widely prevalent. If religion is practised correctly it can never be the cause of tension. Building upon the foundation of Western psychology which gives primacy to the physical urges, we can say that there is some divine urge in us too. The ancient rishis told us about this from their personal experience just as psychologists formulated their theories on personal experience. The rishis told us that we are the children of immortal bliss. Would it not be better to emphasise this divine heritage in us rather than be bogged down by constant preoccupation with the biological dimension of existence?

To get to the essence of religious lessons we should understand that religion does not teach us to suppress our desires. That religion which tells us to suppress desire is not true religion. Here I would like to tell you of an incident in which a similar problem was presented to Sri Ramakrishna by one of his direct disciples, Hari Maharaj, later Swami Turiyananda. It occurred before Hari Maharaj became a full-fledged monk. He had just started visiting Sri Ramakrishna in the Dakshineswar Kali temple near Calcutta. As a young man, Hari Maharaj was at that time subject to severe mental tension. It is a sign of the greatness of this monk that he was frank and open. Though he had accepted Sri Ramakrishna as his master he was up against tremendous mental struggle. His biological urge was powerful. Therefore he went to Sri

Ramakrishna and asked him, "Sir, how can I get rid of lust?"

In this way without attempting to suppress his feelings, Hari Maharaj confessed to his Master frankly. He wanted to realise God but the struggle within him prevented him from making progress. He was assailed by lustful thoughts, his flesh dominated over his spirit and he was at a loss to know what to do.

Sri Ramakrishna heard his question and replied, "It does not go. It is better you give it a different direction." Ramakrishna explained that lust does not leave the flesh till one realises God. The aspirant has to find an alternate channel for it, to recycle it, so to say.

In this context we are reminded of Swami Virajanandaji's injunction. Swami Virajanandaji, the sixth President of the Ramakrishna Order, was a great mystic who realised God. In his book *Paramartha Prasanga* or *Towards the Goal Supreme* he said that "there is no other enemy so formidable and unconquerable as this enemy of lust or kama (desires of the flesh)."

Lust is therefore inevitable, as it is impossible to wipe out the desires of the flesh completely.

But the corrective to this is to give a Godward direction to lust. When we feel desire, we should desire to seek the sweet company of the Lord. If we want to be angry, be angry with Him and say, "Why don't you reveal Yourself to me?"

Let us take Sri Ramakrishna as our model in this matter. He used to say to Mother Kali, "If you are a dead stone, then what is the use of worshipping you? If you are a living reality then reveal yourself." We should emulate his example and be angry in this way. This would be akin to giving a different direction to our lustful nature because it is not possible to obliterate it completely.

Psychologists too never ask us to suppress our desires. If we attempt to suppress our desires the result is unbearable tension and we are likely to be victims of neurotic behaviour and develop various complexes. But there is a problem with Freudian psychologists because they believe that religion teaches us to suppress our desires thereby giving rise to mental conflicts.

This belief is not true. Such a belief does great injustice to our saints and realised souls. The mystics and seers admit that there are powerful urges but at the same time they declare that it is possible to sublimate them. There is also scope for their fulfilment.

A close look at our scriptures reveals that our rishis made provisions for all temperaments. According to them the *chaturvargas—dharma, artha, kama* and *moksha* are all necessary. The first criterion is to lead a righteous life, that is, adherence to *dharma*. Holding on to it as the pillar of life we can earn money by honest, legitimate means. They have also not denied *kama*, sexual urge. If we have lustful desires, it is better to fulfil them; but what we should avoid is being bestial, totally engrossed in them, thinking of pleasure as the ultimate aim of life. Desires can be fulfilled but it should be done with some amount of self-restraint. Once we practice discipline in this matter we shall outgrow this stage and then the aim will be to attain *moksha*.

It is evident that our rishis, as our modern psychologists, made provisions for the existence and expression of desires, but for the former it was only a means and not an end. That means, we are to sublimate all our baser urges and desires and not suppress them.

In this way we must not forget that in addition to our lustful, biological urges we also have a divine dimension in us. If we make life revolve around the former we become no better than animals. But if we make the divine spark come alive then there is the possibility that we shall overcome our animal nature and move towards the divine plane of existence.

Therefore, taking a view contrary to Freud and his followers we can assert that religion when rightly understood helps to dissolve tension instead of creating it. It is dangerous to suppress desires because in that case there is the possibility that they will come to the surface of the mind and make their presence felt sooner or later. Hidden in the depth of the unconscious they might surface in the form of bodily diseases such as stomach ulcers, palpitation of the heart and such others.

Thus it is essential to emphasise that if religion is properly understood, it will strike at the very root of tension. But for this it has to be practised in everyday life. Real religion teaches us that if we are always on the finite plane of existence we shall not be able to overcome mental tension. It also tells us that the pursuit of pleasure cannot be the be-all and end-all of life. A certain amount of mundane pleasure is necessary but we have to go beyond that.

Pleasure should not be mistaken as the ultimate aim of life. The lesson is that we should be able to sublimate these lower desires and make it subordinate to the ultimate desire, meaning the desire to realise the divinity within us. We should know that there is a dimension above the animal level and this dimension should be manifested through self-effort. If the gross pleasures of the body are made the primary objective of life, there is bound to be tension. This is so because such desires stimulate the mind to go for more and more which in turn causes mental conflict and tension.

Of course, religion can also be wrongly perceived and the result is tension. There are some unwise religious teachers who erroneously emphasise the sense of imperfection, guilt and sin in the human make-up. They put this in such exaggerated terms that if we follow their teachings we are sure to end up with mental disturbances. What we require is genuine religious tenets preached by a competent teacher who can show us the positive side of religion.

In this connection what Sri Ramakrishna said is very significant. In one incident in the *Gospel of Sri Ramakrishna* we come across his words saying, "Will you please tell me one thing? Why do you harp so much on sin? By repeating a hundred times 'I am a sinner,' one verily becomes a sinner. One should have such faith as to be able to say, 'What! I have taken the name of God, how can I be a sinner?"

Similar are the words of Swami Vivekananda. In one context he said, "Do not talk of the wickedness of the world and all it sees. The world is made weaker and weaker every day by such teachings. Men are taught from childhood that they are weak and sinners. Teach men that they are the children of immortal bliss. Even those who are the weakest in manifestation, let positive, strong, helpful thoughts enter their brains from the very childhood. Let your lives open to those thoughts and not to weakening and paralysing ones."

These significant words of world teachers such as Sri Ramakrishna and Swami Vivekananda prove that if religion is properly viewed, it will redeem rather than cause mental tension. Instead of emphasising the negative aspects of life we should always speak of the positive aspects. Once more we take recourse to the words of Swami Vivekananda who said, "Who says that we are born sinners? It is a sin to call a man a sinner." This implies that if there are evil tendencies in us let us not be obsessed by them. Let us be aware of the fact that just as the evil is there we also have within us something divine. The aim should be to manifest this divinity in order to neutralise the evil. Viewed thus, the highest truths of religion cannot create stress or tension, nor do they emphasise sinfulness. Instead, they give us a feeling of hope, inspiration, and encouragement for the attainment of a harmonious life.

We need also to discuss the role of *samskaras* as the cause of mental tension. There are certain *samskaras* in us stored during our previous lives according to Hindu thinkers such as Patanjali and Swami Vivekananda. Whatever we are doing now is adding to this store which is often situated in the unconscious region of the mind. We have both good and bad *samskaras* in us— each person is a bundle of *shubh* (auspicious) and *ashubh* (inauspicious) *samskaras*. If we are inclined towards bad deeds it shows that the *samskaras* we have acquired in the past—during this life and in earlier ones—are bad. But there is a significant point here which is noteworthy: our thinkers have declared that since we are given freedom, if we are a prey to bad tendencies we can undo them by cultivating good *samskaras*. As we begin to cultivate good *samskaras*, the process of elimination of bad *samskaras* goes on simultaneously. In other words, there is every scope for improving ourselves with the help of the free will that has been given to human beings. Hindu thinkers are not fatalistic. They are dynamic, progressive and their message brings hope to humanity.

Another point to note is about environment. We are placed in a congenial environment; suddenly, in spite of our best efforts we are swept off our feet by unacceptable emotions. This happens because of the presence of our previous *ashubh samskaras*. Having recognised this we have to exercise our self-effort to overcome them. As has been rightly pointed out, man is the architect of his own destiny. Our approach should be that if I am prone to bad actions at present, I also have something divine in me. If I can tap that resource and undo the evil, it will help me to have a better future.

Further, from the Freudian point of view, mental tension is said to be very difficult to overcome unless there is a resolution of the conflict between the unconscious, biological urge for pleasure and the imposition of certain amount of control, restraint and censorship by the super-ego. To nullify this conflict we have to cultivate a real religious attitude.

But recent reflections on the Freudian school of psychology have propagated the idea that even if all impositions of censorship by the super-ego are removed mental tension still remains. They believe that it is not possible to remove the conflict completely and this is the cause of stress. For instance, if a person goes with a TV or VCR to a jungle to enjoy it where there are no kinds of restraints, he still finds that he is not totally free. He has checks from within. His inner voice tells him that he is disintegrating his self, that he is destroying himself. Unless a person is a brute, this voice will haunt him. Therefore, the ultimate censorship is not external, it is the highest form of censorship, a person's *viveka*. As a great swami has said, "the voice of conscience is the voice of God." When there is no outside check, our own mind, or something within us, tells us what is wrong.

Even if we go into the solitude of a jungle to enjoy ourselves and get immersed in degrading pleasures, to plunge ourselves into the lowest abyss, we shall not be free of tensions. In such cases we have to admit that external factors are not the sole causes of tensions. It is our inherent desires for satisfaction, those impelled by our biological and other urges that result in tensions.

Tensions are also created by a wrong understanding of life in general. Unless we lead a balanced, integrated life and have a right attitude to the meaning of existence, we are prone to mental tensions. It is true that frustration of certain urges causes tension; but the moment we perceive these urges in the right perspective we shall find a cure to our tension.

Mental tension is also common in people who have a strong urge for self-expression. This is a general phenomenon in people who develop peculiar behavioural patterns when their urge is denied. They take the path of revolt. For instance, if parents place restrictions on their children according to what they feel will benefit the children, the latter always revolt. They feel that their freedom is being unnecessarily curtailed. When the father says, "Don't watch so much television," the child is inclined to watch more of it. The children resent these impositions of limitations. As they grow older the urge for self-expression becomes stronger. There are innumerable examples of adolescent children acting contrary to the ideas and ideals of their parents. It is upto the parents to understand the psychological requirements of their children and deal with them accordingly. When children feel that they are always kept under control, thwarted or frustrated in their attempt to do anything, they are bound to rebel. This can be averted if the parents are a little tactful. They should sympathise with the children's desire for self-expression and try not to come in their way so that serious trouble is avoided. Unless the urge for self-expression is given a certain amount of scope, it creates abnormalities in the mind.

Another factor which causes mental tension is the great emotional urge we call ambition. A person who has an indomitable urge for power, position or intellectual achievements often finds that he is unable to compete with others to get what he wants, or someone already has what he covets and he thus becomes very apprehensive. He despairs of getting what he wants and suffers from incurable stress. For instance, take the example of headship in the various departments of a university. Nowadays this position is given by rotation so there is not much problem. In case this rule is revoked, it will cause unimaginable tension among the professors in the various departments. A person may feel that he has better credentials to occupy the position but the university authorities are not giving him due recognition for his excellence. In other words, ambition creates unlimited anxiety and tension.

One often notices these days that young scholars become mentally sick and disturbed due to excessive ambition. They develop functional ailments and show neurotic behaviour. Scholars who are a prey to anxiety and neurosis are the ones who want to go further and further beating their competitors. When their desires are not fulfilled, they suffer from acute mental tension. In this way, ambition for position, recognition or appreciation becomes a source of tension.

Among causes for tension one more item is intellectualism which can also create tension. Let me explain the term with an example. Suppose a person is born in a family of scholars where everyone is highly educated, post-graduates and doctorates. All have a brilliant academic record. But this person is not academically brilliant though he has a flair for something else. Such a person may think, "If I pursue a career of my own choice, what will my family feel! I have been born in a family of scholars. If I do not achieve academic excellence, my life will be miserable." He will thus try to imitate the others and create tension for himself. But he can cure himself if he thinks, "I have been born with a different kind of temperament. I have a special aptitude. I will prove my excellence in that field. It is not necessary for me to prove myself academically as good as my father or grandfather." In this way if he proceeds according to his aptitude he can have a happy, satisfying and fulfilling life.

Ambition can lead us to over-work and it is certain that if a person is over-worked he must suffer from tension. A person who has many responsibilities, gives himself no time to rest due to over-riding ambition or some other motive is constantly under terrible tension. In this way even the so-called higher values which are laudable and have social sanction may result in various types of imbalances leading to great mental stress.

Chapter 3

Some Views about Mental Tension

Let us now consider what Carl Gustav Jung, one of the eminent modern psycho-analysts has to say about the causes of mental tension. According to Jung, tension is created by the double nature of human beings—masculine and feminine. Let me explain what he meant by this: by "masculine" he meant extrovert, and by "feminine" he meant introvert. In this world we find people who are by nature extroverts, who always have an outgoing tendency and do not know how to lead an inner life. As against this, there are introverts. According to Jung, tension is a result of these two opposite tendencies— extrovert and introvert—working against each other in a single individual. What is the remedy to this tension?

The remedy is that we must have a

harmonious blending of the active aspect of life
with the contemplative one. Leading an active
life without devoting time to contemplation or
inwardness may create havoc. Again, constant
meditation alone without going through the
usual procedures of learning the correct path
from a true guru may also lead to mental
imbalance. We have to strike a balance, adopt
the middle path, so to say. We have to be active
and at the same time we must have time for a
little meditation, introspection and self-analysis.
By a harmonious blending of these two opposite
tendencies—masculine and feminine, extrovert
and introvert—we can get rid of mental tension.

Take the case of different people of this
world - people of wealth, power, position and
such others. If we look into their lives we find a
great number of people—wealthy, or
powerful—greatly disturbed because they have
not been able to reach the higher dimensions of
existence. Unless our inner nature is satisfied,
we will never be free from mental tension.

Often a question comes to our mind: Are all
religious people contented? Does it mean that
those who take *diksha* or perform different
ritualistic exercises have been able to overcome

tension? Is it not a fact, let us admit frankly, that even people practising meditation often suffer from mental tension?

For instance, suppose a person is in a particular mood and is sitting in a temple or a shrine. If you go to him, he says rudely, "Don't disturb me. I am now meditating."

Well, if you are really successful in meditation, it means that at that time you are in communion with your higher nature. When you come back from your room or the temple, you should be a changed person. At least, we expect a sweet, cordial behavior from you. But it has been our experience that people who do the so-called meditation, sometimes become very violent. It shows that they do not know how to practise real spiritual discipline. We may conclude that if religious life is lived correctly people will always be satisfied, they will become calm and collected.

Anybody coming into contact with a truly religious person will feel the peaceful vibrations that emanate from such a person. We will think, "here is a calm and collected man. We don't find any mental disturbances in him." But if we go to a person who is himself suffering from different kinds of agitation, we will naturally get a different kind of vibration. All this means that even if we do not have genuine realisation of the inner truth, if through meditation we can have a glimpse of the higher self in us, then real meditation will go a long way in overcoming our mental tension.

And that is the reason why we find in Swami Vivekananda's conception of the emblem of the Ramakrishna Mission, a harmonious blending of all the four yogas. Unlike Jung who merely suggested a balance of the masculine and the feminine temperaments, that is, action and contemplation, Swami Vivekananda, a true rishi, following the tradition of our great masters, has gone further and suggested a harmonious blending of the four yogas in a comprehensive visual form.

Those who are familiar with the emblem of the Ramakrishna Mission and have studied and analysed it carefully find that there is a lotus in the centre which stands for devotion; a rising sun stands for *jnana* or wisdom; a serpent for psychic control, that is, *Raja Yoga*; and the waves stand for *karma*. In the emblem we also find a swan which stands for our divine soul or *Paramatman*. The idea is that through a harmonious blending of *Raja Yoga, Karma Yoga, Jnana Yoga* and *Bhakti Yoga* we are able to realise the *Paramatman* in us. That is the reason Swamiji prescribed this new yoga—*Samanvaya Yoga*—because in the present day world all of us have to lead an extremely hectic life. Before we start our day's work it is ideal to practise the *Samanvaya Yoga* for at least fifteen minutes. After this when we go back to the field of activity we are able to sustain an elevated mood.

Let me illustrate this. Suppose one is an executive or is working in an office, or is a doctor, a professor, a housewife, or something else. Even if we are not initiated devotees, even if we have not taken *diksha* from anybody, we can surely practise a little introspection in the morning at least. When we try to exercise psychic control of the mind it is *Raja Yoga*. We are told that man is not finite, that behind this limited frame there is a divine spark. We try to be in tune with that divine nature by exercising mental, psychic control. That means we are doing a little of *Raja Yoga*.

Then, once we are back to work, suppose as a housewife one does household chores, we must love the work which has been given to us.

If there is no love for the work it ceases to be work, it becomes a drudgery. Now the person who acts with love is in the state of *Bhakti Yoga*. We may not go to a temple with flowers and incense sticks in the traditional sense of *bhakti* but we have this devotional attitude through the grace of the Almighty, that whatever work we do we are able to look on it with love and devotion. That is *Bhakti Yoga*, working with *shraddha*.

When we come into contact with numerous people in the course of the day—family, friends, colleagues, students if one is a professor, patients if one is a doctor, if our attitude to all of them is similar that there is the same *Paramatman* in all, then we are discriminating between the eternal and the non-eternal. There is something eternal behind everyone, it is a recognition of man's divine nature. From the individual standpoint it is the *Atman*, from the universal it is the *Brahman*. In this way we are led to the practice of discrimination which is *Jnana Yoga*.

Again when we work, if we do it without any ulterior motive, that is, work for work's sake, that is *Karma Yoga*. Swami Vivekananda said that we may do hundreds of jobs but we should not let the work produce a single ripple in the mind. We should perform all actions with an attitude of non-attachment to the results.

In this way everyday we are able to include the four types of yoga in our schedule. That is *Samanvaya Yoga*. In the morning before we begin the day's work we are *raja yogis*. We begin our work with devotion and take up the attitude of a *bhakti yogi*. While working with or for others we practice discrimination and are *jnana yogis*, and finally we do all the tasks assigned to us in the spirit of *karma yogis*.

Unless we adopt these attitudes, we are sure to react adversely to whatever incident takes place. For instance, if a subordinate insults a person, he will reply in kind unless he keeps in mind the innate divinity of the subordinate which makes them equals on the spiritual plane. This is possible only through rigorous self-analysis which is called *Jnana Yoga*. To be a successful practitioner of *Samanvaya Yoga* we have to constantly check whether we are exhibiting the right attitudes of mind.

In our earlier discussions we have given much importance to the causes of mental tension. To cope with it we usually do a variety of things. But much of it is only palliative. For example, medical treatment is often given to us based on certain external symptoms but it does little for the underlying, deep seated malady which is not manifest in any visible form.

Suppose a person is suffering from acute mental tension and is terribly upset. If he has the habit of smoking, he would like to smoke his tension away; others might take intoxicants, aspirin or sleeping tablets, watch television or go for an outing or on a vacation. Each practises relaxation in his or her own way but they have very little success in overcoming the actual cause of the tension or stress.

Let me repeat that nervous tension is a kind of psychosomatic disease. There is general agreement that a greater number of our diseases are psychosomatic—both physical and mental. And they influence our thoughts, our prejudices, our beliefs, our environment and also how we react to different situations. Of course, this does not mean that symptoms of various diseases such as ulcer or headache are all imaginary. Certainly not.

Suppose someone has a headache and I say "Why are you taking a pain-killer? The headache is imaginary." Such a comment is unkind because if a person is suffering we must believe him and not think his pain is imaginary. The point is: why does the headache occur? There must be a cause. Diseases of various kinds are real enough. To designate them as 'psychosomatic' is to acknowledge that the major cause of a disease is a person's emotional stress. We all suffer from emotional stress or tension. In other words, the way we react to our environment results in some kinds of internal psychological changes which evolve into some kind of disease of the body.

The pattern for all these diseases, of course, is different. Suppose a person is a victim of anger. Instead of giving expression to his anger he suppresses it. This may develop into mental depression or migraine - headache. Even though the development of a specific psychosomatic disease is unique in each individual, the underlying principle is the same.

We have to carefully see what this underlying principle is. We allow ourselves to be swayed by different kinds of emotions and as a result of the emotional stress we subject ourselves to psychological stress. In this way emotional stress leads to an eventual breakdown of our organic system.

A classic example is ulcer. Obviously it has a connection with nervous tension. One of the characteristics typically associated with ulcer is a tendency to exaggerate worries, or find it difficult to express feelings of anger and fear openly. The other day a person came to me and said, "Swamiji, I am seized with fear, fear of cancer. I don't know why this fear has possessed me. I know in my saner moments that I am all right. Still the thought that I have cancer does not leave me. It has no remedy."

Such a situation is often encountered when we have a high degree of competitiveness or a tendency to exaggerate worries. Poor dietary habits such as eating when one is tense or eating quickly may result in what the doctors term as an overly acidic condition in the gastrointestinal track which ultimately results in ulcer. This malady could have been prevented had it been attended to earlier by taking into account the patient's emotional stress. The tension under which he/she had been labouring should have been handled with care. Then perhaps we could have prevented the ulcer.

What is thus needed is to pay careful attention to a patient's personal history from which we can invariably trace the origin of psychosomatic diseases back to patterns of emotional pressures. This instance of ulcer is just one among the variety of psychosomatic diseases. Many more examples can be given, all of which are directly related to some kind of nervous stress or tension. Even common diseases like headache, which I have already mentioned, in addition to cold, backache, chest pain are all psychosomatic. It is difficult to predict accurately why some organs are more affected by stress than others. But one thing which modern medical science has made effectively clear is that nervous tension or stress is at the root of all psychosomatic diseases, regardless of the organic system involved.

Modern research is also beginning to reveal a direct relationship between nervous tension and what is called in medical parlance, CVD (Cardio Vascular Disease). According to the latest data, strokes and heart diseases are the greatest killers and nervous tension is most often the basis of these diseases. In this area, the relationship between nervous tension and CVD is clearly described by Dr. Mayer Friedman and Dr. Ray Rosenman in their monumental work entitled "Type A Behaviour and your Fear." In it they point out that there are certain personalities called type A personalities who are very much prone to Cardio Vascular Diseases. And there is another type known as type B who are not so prone to it as type A is.

Regarding the characteristics of a type A personality, we can say that such a person is almost always under constant pressure to perform. They have their mind filled with the idea that they have to do the job in hand because no one else will be able to do it. This is the reason why such a person is engulfed by pressure.

A person who is under constant pressure to perform is in a hurry to do everything. Such a person is also characterised by impatience, driving ambition, endless desire for competing, aggressiveness and quite often hostility too. He/she seems to be always short of time and the twenty-four hours of a day seem insufficient. There is a feeling that they have too much to do. But in this process of overcrowding themselves they have created psychological problems and health hazards for themselves.

On the other hand, type B personalities

appear to be calm and relaxed and free from the desperate urgency of fighting against time. Such persons do not harbour much anger. They know when to relax and enjoy themselves. Statistically such a personality does not have much danger of contacting CVD.

It is often thought by type A personalities that they can do more than the type B ones who do not get excited and do their work in a calm and quiet manner. But the fact is that the former do not achieve more than the latter for the simple reason that they dissipate much energy in useless pressures. The type B persons work silently and in a relaxed manner which produces effective results.

The busy executive is a classic example of type A personality. In some of the characteristics of such a personality already noted, we may elaborate further. He is a person who is engaged in a struggle to obtain optimum conditions or quick results in the shortest possible time. He feels that the work has to be done quickly and often against opposition. He is often under pressure from within to obtain more and more in less time.

In a word, type A personalities feel that they

have to be efficient, they have to prove their efficiency to others. If the target of a particular task is five years they drive themselves hard to finish it a few months ahead of time in order to get credit from the boss. Since the trait of aggressiveness is strong in such a personality and also unlimited ambition, such people are often the ones who are work oriented. Even when left to himself he does not have time to do a little self-analysis. If he is asked to stop working he will go mad. Such a person is often too explicit in speech and has little control over what he is going to say. He focuses his attention exclusively on his work and fails to notice or enjoy the beautiful things in life. We can describe him as permanently tense.

While comparing the types A and B, Dr. Friedman and Dr. Rosenman gave the following chart attributing some typical traits to each of the two types. In the first case, that is type A, we find:

1. Hurried speech.
2. Constant rapid movement in eating.
3. Open impatience.
4. Chronic sense of time urgency.
5. Thinking and performing several things at once.

6. An active attempt to dominate the conversation, to determine the topics, to remain preoccupied with one's thoughts when others are talking.

7. Vague sense of guilt during periods of relaxation when doing nothing.

8. Excessive concern with getting things worth having, no time to become that which is worth being. That means, they are over-concerned about how to get things done but do not reflect upon the fact of how they can become better human beings. Their sole concern is to get the work executed—no compassion for other types of people.

9. They have certain typical gestures, physical nervous gestures, such as clenching fists, grinding teeth, etc.

These are the characteristics of a personality who is prone to heart diseases. As against this is the type B personality who has the following characteristics:

1. No sense of time urgency.

2. No felt need to discuss or display one's achievements and accomplishments unless the situation demands it. That means if somebody

wants it, of course, type B people will speak about their achievements but they do not believe in parading their achievements or boasting about them.

3. A belief that play exists for fun and relaxation, not to exhibit superiority.

4. An ability to relax without guilt.

5. One who can work without any kind of excitement, without any agitation.

Though type A personalities can claim that they are the real *Karma yogis*, yet in the light of the characteristics just enumerated, we can say that a real *Karma yogi* will do everything in a calm and collected manner. As Swami Vivekananda said, "The calmer we are, the less disturbed our nerves will be, the more shall we love and the better our work will be."

Chapter 4

Stress and the Dynamics of Success

The two types of personalities and their characeristics we discussed so far are determinants of behaviour. In any job which we do—as executives, housewives, students, professors, doctors—it is not the work that is primary but the attitudes and behavioural patterns which we bring to it which are important. Our attitude to our experiences determines to which of the two types we belong.

Let me repeat that those who belong to type A, irrespective of gender, are prone to CVD. There are many women all over the world who have actively entered the hitherto male-dominated fields and such women imbibe the characteristics of type A personalities. They are work-oriented, have less patience, always suffer from a sense of time urgency, have no time for relaxation and are also thus prone to CVD. In other words, heart diseases do not discriminate between men and women. It is an opportunistic disease which may afflict all those who follow the life-style of a type A personality.

In this context it would be worthwhile to dwell for a moment on the Vedantic analysis of non-self. In each one of us, both the real self and an apparent self are present. Swami Vivekananda spoke about "Man the Real and Man the Apparent" in one of his famous lectures in the West on Jnana Yoga. For instance, when you look at me and I look at you, what we see is a particular mind-body complex all of which comes under our apparent self. This apparent self is subject to different changes. It is born, grows, develops, decays and dies. This apparent self of ours has many distinctions and *upadhis*; it differentiates each from the other in various respects—sex, language, religion. But, in spite of all these distinctions, at the back of each of us there is the real, permanent self. Therefore, the apparent self implies the non-self and the real self the Atman.

In Vedanta we find a brilliant analysis of the non-self with reference to five different sheaths or *panchakoshas*. We shall study these in detail in another context. We shall once again discuss the type A personality engaged in a ceaseless struggle against time. The result is emotional tension; the type A person has typically a higher level of muscular tension. According to Dr. Friedman and Dr. Rosenman, they are three times more likely to experience heart diseases. The note of warning here is that we should go slow. We should not be excited. We should not do anything on the spur of the moment. What is being emphasised is that those who are cautious and patient are likely to commit less mistakes. In addition they will also be safe from all those diseases which are the result of nervous tension.

In our society, at present, we find the Type A personality in common occurence. Often it is associated with success. The thought process of the type A personality impells him/her thus: "I want to achieve this, I want to achieve that; I have limited time at my disposal. I have to go ahead in life. I have to achieve my goals in the shortest possible time." But actually it has been seen that those who go slow perhaps achieve more tangible results than those who are geared to what may be called short-term results because in the long run this constant pursuit of impossible deadlines is destructive and limiting.

Apart from the two types already mentioned there is another type of personality which also exhibits the ill effects of stress. Since it is unlike type A or B, we can classify it under a different category. In the language of psychology it is called "the helpless and hopeless type." Let us analyse this type.

If we ponder over the name of the category a little carefully, we shall be able to understand it. As the name suggests, the people who belong to this type have a negative approach to life. They fail to perceive the brighter aspects of life. They are totally pessimistic and think that "life is all dark. There is no hope because I am born like that. I can never achieve success." Such a negative mental set-up in the helpless-hopeless type is the cause of his/her suffering. The core belief in such a person is that no matter what he/she does, it is not going to have much effect.

When such a person contracts some illness his first thought is "However much I try I shall never be cured." The doctor assures him that if he follows the treatment properly and takes the medicines regularly he is sure to improve, the patient continues to brood that there is no hope and he is doomed to die. Thus, he always harbours negative thoughts in all contexts. He feels what may be called powerless, caught in an impossible situation. He believes that he has no control over any aspect of his life, his relationship with others or his environment.

People who come under the helpless-hopeless type also suffer from nervous tension due to various reasons. For example, if there is a death in the family, the departure of a beloved person, or a transfer from one post to another, such a person says, "Oh, it is beyond my control. I was all along going in a particular direction but circumstances are against me and now I am stuck in such a way that I cannot come out."

People who are suffering from stress can surely be expected to have too many commitments. It is difficult to fulfill all the commitments and if we try to squeeze numerous activities in our limited time we are bound to suffer from nervous tension. It is easy to visualise that such people feel as if caught in the treadmill of life and always in high gear. But this is not the right attitude to life. Even if a person is somehow able to cope with the situation, sooner or later it will show adverse results and the person will be forced to take recourse to alcohol, or some kind of drug in order to maintain the tremendous tempo of his zeal of going forward. Of couse, the inevitable does overtake them and the person manages to burn himself out soon because of the excessive pressure of excitement and tension.

Here the science of *yoga* seems to me extremely relevant. Since we suffer from mental tension it is natural that we should refer to the workings of the mind. Obviously, when we discuss the mind we are discussing the *manomayakosha*. When I say that people with numerous commitments burn themselves out, I speak of the *pranic* energy or the *pranamayakosha* and the body which ultimately wears out is called the *annamayakosha* or the physical sheath.

According to the science of Yoga, human beings are made up of various levels called sheaths. We are all basically *Atman*—pure consciousness—but our first or grossest covering is this physical frame or the *annamayakosha*. Within this body or sheath, the *annamayakosha*, there is something subtler called the *pranamayakosha*. We can see and touch the physical body but we cannot do the same with the *pranic* body. Of course, we can feel its action such as the moving of a hand, making a speech, etc. The energy level of the *pranamayakosha* makes these actions possible. If the *prana* goes out of the body it dies. Fasting at a stretch for twenty days may reduce the body to a skeleton and the person may even die. But as soon as a little fruit or juice or milk is given to the body the *pranic* energy or vitality returns.

Thus the subtle energy maintains the gross physical body. Again, the subtle level of the *pranamayakosha* is maintained by the level of the mind, the *manomayakosha*. In case a decision has to be made we have to go beyond these three levels to the next *kosha* known as the *Vijnanamayakosha*. This will be discussed in detail later. Let us first discuss the three levels—*annamayakosha*, *pranamayakosha* and *manomayakosha*.

Referring once again to our discussion of the helpless-hopeless type we can recall that such a personality's negative mental make up is based on the core belief that whatever he may do, the situation will not change for the better. The sense of hopelessness they suffer from is impossible to overcome. For instance, if a student constantly broods and is depressed, he will never be brilliant. He refuses to study or put in hard work because all his time is spent in complaining that he is incapable of achieving a good result.

I recollect an incident in my own life at the time I was appearing for my M.A. examination in Philosophy of the Calcutta University in the year 1950. The venue was the famous Senate Hall. One of my batchmates, Jyotirmaya Hore, a very brilliant student was sitting beside me during the examination. On the third day the question paper was extremely tough. After some time he muttered to me, "I am leaving the hall. The questions are terribly difficult. I know I cannot get a first class." I said, "You are brilliant. Don't leave the hall. Keep up your spirit and try once more." He refused to listen to me. He was labouring under a feeling of hopelessness. He left the examination hall and had to pay a heavy price for it. Naturally he lost a year. Again the next year too he could not get a first class. The first time he appeared he got first class marks in all the papers but failed to write one paper.

If he had displayed a little patience and perseverance, his result would have been good. But his "helpless and hopeless" attitude was the cause of his downfall.

It is obvious that hopelessness leads to a decrease in or withdrawal of mental energy. When a doctor prescribes a medicine only a patient who is hopeful of recovery and has sufficient mental energy will benefit by it. Often it happens that a father encourages his son to study well but in case the boy suffers from this feeling of hopelessness his mental energy will slowly decline. This is what happened to my friend of the M.A. days. It was the failure of his mental energy which showed itself in the form of his lack of determination and made him leave the examination hall.

Such a thing did happen to me too when we had to face that tough paper at the M.A. examination. I was completely taken aback by the questions which no one expected. My first thought was to follow my friend Hore. Had I done so I think I would never have completed my post graduation. Life took a different direction and I became a monk immediately after that. Had I walked out of the hall I may not even have had the opportunity to become a monk. One wrong decision would have wrecked my whole life.

The duration of that examination was four hours. Fifteen minutes had gone in thinking what to do. Then I looked at the essays and thought that I should at least try to attempt one of them. I knew that all the other students were in the same plight which gave me courage and I made up my mind to try answering at least one question. Suddenly my *pranic* energy came back and took me above the feeling of hopelessness. In turn the energy travelled from the *pranamaya* to the *manomaya* and then to the *vijnanamaya koshas* because I could arrive at the correct decision.

There are times when our mind cannot decide and the next level called the *buddhi* (intellect) takes over. The *buddhi* has the deciding faculty. It enables us to make the correct decision. I can say that during that difficult examination at the Senate Hall, I appealed to my *vijnanamayakosha*. I attempted an essay on the Concept of the Dynamic Absolute and in this paper I got very good marks! I had prepared a particular essay which did not figure in the question paper. This gave rise to the feeling of despair which I had to overcome. Physically I was fine, that is as far as the *annamayakosha* was concerned, there was no problem. The *pranic* energy was also present because I had come prepared to write an examination. I needed that *pranavayu* but the mind was not able to make a decision. Then I had to appeal to the *vijnanamayakosha* to give me a decision.

When I began to write, half an hour was gone and only three and a half hours were left in which I had to complete the four hour essay. But there was a valuable lesson in this experience. Later I always advised students never to give up hope when such things happen. Instead they should always take a positive attitude. Situations can be overcome without losing hope, without succumbing to hopelessness. As I have said from my own experience, the body was alright. Had I been sick I could not have appeared for the examination. The *pranic* energy was also in abundance because I finished a four hour paper in three and a half hours. Mental energy was there and it helped me to appeal to the *vijnanamayakosha* for making the right decision.

After the examination I left the result to the Almighty with the satisfaction that I had done justice to the topic - Concept of the Dynamic Absolute.

In other words, hope makes energy active and hopelessness leads to a decrease in or withdrawal of energy. If we give up hope we shall not have sufficient energy to do any work. My friend Hore gave up hope and his brain had no energy to function. His *manomaya* and *vijnanamaya koshas* failed to help him; *pranic* energy fell and as a result he left the hall. When the body field or the *annamayakosha* is no longer correctly maintained the finer supportive fields such as the *manomaya* and *pranamayakosha* are weakened. Therefore the natural processes of decay are accelerated and disease may readily occur.

Often this phenomenon of the decaying process of our energy is specific. For example, a physician who practises what in these days is called holistic medicine once related to me the case of a woman with significant degenerative eye disease. On enquiry it was found out that at the root of the degeneration was the patient's unwillingness to look at things. She always suffered from a feeling of hopelessness. The ultimate physical malady of cancer in her eye was not a sudden phenomenon. It was the effect of specific mental disruption. In such instances there is a withdrawal of mental energy and subsequently the organ's specific reduction of the energy field.

To counter this the science of Yoga talks about two more levels or sheaths that support the mind-energy-body complex. One is called the wisdom sheath or the *vijnanamayakosha*, the experience of a higher mind with intuition as mentioned earlier. Sometimes intuition is also insufficient, therefore we refer to the final blissful sheath or *anandamayakosha* which deals with transcendental consciousness.

These two sheaths, that is the *vijnanamayakosha* and the *anandamayakosha* are what may be called the subtle body or *sukshma sharira*. It follows that when there are certain disruptions like the times when we cease to find meaning in life or suffer from feelings of hopelessness or helplessness we need these levels. Naturally in such cases we can take it for granted that there are corresponding imbalances in the mind-body-energy complex, that is the *pranamaya-manomaya-annamayakoshas.*

To explain the meaning of *sukshma sharira* we should refer to Vedanta so that it can be easily understood. To recapitulate, *annamayakosha* is the gross physical body. It consists of bones, flesh and so on. It exists and it dies. *Pranamayakosha* is that which activates all organs of action; it refers to the five organs of action. When the mind is united with the five organs of knowledge, it is called *manomayakosha*; and when *buddhi* is connected with the five organs of knowledge it is called *vijnanamayakosha*; and the final sheath of consciousness is the *anandamayakosha*.

Atman is covered by all these five sheaths. They are called sheaths because they conceal the nature of the Atman, as a sheath covers a knife or sword. But the Atman which is beyond these *panchakoshas* is completely detached from all these coverings.

The five layers mentioned above can well be compared to the five layers of clouds. When the sun is shining and dense clouds come to obstruct the vision of the effulgent sun we are unable to see the rays of the sun and say that there is no sun. Similarly we cannot comprehend the presence of the Atman within us on account of the clouds of impurities of this life and innumerable past lives and say that there is no Atman. We live under tremendous delusion. We commit the same mistake as when the sky is overcast and we deny the very existence of the sun.

When there is only a thin layer of cloud the sun is partially visible as is the case of the *anandamayakosha* which is the closest to the Atman, so to say. The light that shines through these different layers differs in degree depending on the density of the clouds. If the cloud is a little thicker, it is like the *vijnanamayakosha*, still thicker - it is the *manomayakosha*, thicker than that, it is like the *pranamayakosha* and an absolute covering is the *annamayakosha*.

A person who identifies himself with the gross physical body will never have illumination. The self when identified with the mind creates doubt. A thinker is a doubter. The *vijnanamayakosha* or the sheath of *buddhi* is called the discriminating faculty and is finer than the mind. It is close to the *anandamayakosha* and is the sheath of intellect which helps to arrive at a decision or to achieve certainty. To achieve certainty therefore, the Atman uses the sheath of intellect. The sheath of intellect or *buddhi* is extremely effulgent because of its proximity to the Supreme Self. Through the fifth and final sheath of bliss *anandamayakosha* one experiences varying degrees of happiness. The chief features of this sheath are rest and joy such as we experience when we come into contact with an agreeable object. A fuller manifestation of the sheath of bliss is experienced in deep sleep. After waking from sleep a person may remark that he slept happily.

These five sheaths are all modifications of matter. The sheath of bliss is closest to the Atman but it is not Atman itself. Like the other sheaths it is endowed with changing attributes whereas the Atman is changeless. All the five sheaths have no permanent reality. Whatever reality they are perceived to possess is due to the fact that Atman is their substratum. The real glory of the Atman is unobstructed by any sheath. Through discrimination and non-attachment, self-control and meditation, a person no longer identifies himself with any of the sheaths but remains constantly absorbed in the Self. Our goal should be to make the sheaths thinner and more transparent through *japa sadhana, sadhu sanga*, discrimination and such other acts. When there are no more obstructing clouds we shall be face to face with the truth.

From this brief analysis of the different sheaths we come to the conclusion that to overcome mental tension one has to take recourse to disciplines and remain in complete communion with the Self. We suffer from tension because we attach reality to the sheaths. Rising above these and trying to be absorbed in our own Self is a cure to outside agitations, excitements. Once we admit the reality of the Self these external upheavals cannot touch us.

Finally let us recall the words of Sri Ramakrishna. He used to say that a person's bondage is in the mind and liberation is also in the mind. If the mind is *suddha* or pure, a person can realise the Atman. If the mind is covered with impurities it is not possible to realise the self-shining Atman within. All problems of the mind are summed up in this important idea.

Chapter 5

World View in Relation to Mental States

People who are vulnerable to the feeling of hopelessness often have a mechanistic view of the world. They feel that they cannot avoid the inexorable nature of fate and destiny which have their own inevitable course. There is nothing that can be done by them, they feel. Because they suffer with the feeling of hopelessness, they are under the impression that good things in life are rare and when they do come it is only through extreme hard work. For ordinary or mediocre people there is no hope of any good. They doubt their ability which serves as a block preventing them from finding outlets for their emotions.

There are different phases of hopelessness. According to LeShan the early experiences, beliefs and thought patterns of some individuals are responsible for the development of the first phase of hopelessness. Then there is a second phase where a person accepts whatever is given and tries to fulfil his duties without innovation and ingenuity. The third phase is where a meaningful relationship or a satisfying job is suddenly terminated and the person becomes a victim of hopelessness.

For instance, a person had an important position in a particular field. Suddenly he is transferred to another field. To begin with he is able to find satisfaction in his new assignment; but sooner or later he may think that he is not getting adequate satisfaction out of the new job he has been given. This results gradually in utter despair. In the categorisation of LeShan these people belong to the third phase of hopelessness. They hold a totally negative view of themselves and the world. They have the following beliefs:

1. Objects and people outside of themselves cannot bring any help.

2. There is no possibility of development or change. They firmly believe that things will remain bad for them and there are no more

bright prospects for them.

3. They think that even if they are given some other work it also will not relieve them of their loneliness.

Interestingly, though these individuals suffer from acute hopelessness, they continue to function. They may only be passing through a phase of hopelessness. It does not mean that under its influence they give up their jobs or give up living. On the surface they appear placid and hardworking, but behind all this they are convinced that there is no hope for them. They feel that they have achieved whatever they had to do and there is no further possibility of achievement in life. Consequently they feel entrapped. In the words of LeShan, "There are cases when this feeling of hopelessness sometimes leads to the fatal disease called cancer."

LeShan describes a typical case of a lady Jenny. When he approached her she was on her death bed. She had terminal cancer. When he asked her about her experiences and how she developed cancer she said in a quiet voice, "Well, I am not surprised at it because from the beginning I had a feeling that there was no hope for me and I would never have real happiness in life."

This illustrates how from the very beginning Jenny adopted a negative attitude and made herself a victim of the fatal disease. Some of the typical experiences which induce hopelessness are the death of a spouse or a family member, loss of a high position or power, a threat, or such other causes. If these adverse conditions come up in the life of a person who has all along lived an integrated life, a deeply spiritual life and has always cultivated some fundamental positive virtues such a person will not have this kind of negative thinking. But those who lack this dimension in life are always heard grumbling, "Oh, why did God destine this for me? I am going to die. There is no hope. What will happen to my family after me? I wish God would take me quickly. I cannot bear this suffering any more. Why is He not taking me to His abode?" and such others.

Illness, hospitalisation, etc. on the one hand and retirement from a job on the other, is another thing which makes a person give in to a sense of hopelessness. Unless a retired person has some other meaningful engagement he develops a negative attitude towards life. There are a fortunate few who feel happy to retire, thinking that they have worked hard for long enough and are now ready to enjoy their leisure. Some people come to us and say that they would like to offer some voluntary service. There are many such people engaged in the day-to-day administration of the different centres of the Ramakrishna Mission.

But people for whom life was going on smoothly as long as they were in active service suddenly fail to adjust to retirement and wonder what they should do with their time. They develop a sense of hopelessness. Another instance is when a person is assigned inferior work. Perhaps the authorities do him an injustice. It may be work that is perceived as demeaning or causes loss of physical independence, or ultimately leads to some kind of chronic physical pain, say acute asthma, etc. There is bound to be a feeling of hopelessness.

Keeping in mind these causes of hopelessness which ultimately lead to nervous tension, J. F. Muller has suggested a progression in the development of hopelessness in which a person increasingly fails to reach the goals.

However much he tries, he can never arrive at a possible solution and gradually loses faith in himself. This gives way to utter despair where everything appears dark and there are no bright prospects.

Such a person gradually withdraws from all kinds of social relationships, loses sleep, has no appetite and all his energy *pranamayakosha* is drained out. He finds it difficult to make decisions through *manomayakosha* and may turn to drugs or intoxicating drinks for solace and relief. But they find no solace and are caught inexorably in the web of hopelessness.

An eminent writer G. L. Engel describes this feeling of hopelessness as "the giving-up-given-up complex". Some of the special features which are characteristically exhibited by such people are:

1. They always feel that one is at the end of all hope—at a block or impasse. They cannot remove the block and proceed further.

2. They have a poor self image. They think they are not competent enough. In their underestimating of themselves they are full of negative thoughts. As a result everything goes out of their control.

3. The third feature according to Engel is that such a person begins to feel a   lack of gratification from the role he has to play. He no longer has job satisfaction.

4. Such a person feels that there is no continuity between past, present and   future. Past memories of hopelessness plague him. He continues to brood   over them and this results in suffering.

Helplessness may also be considered as a spiritual impasse. When a person loses faith in himself he perceives life as meaningless and thinks that there is no hope for self-expression.

In this connection I am reminded of the words of a Buddhist monk. His name is Tarthang Tulku Rimpoche, a Tibetian Buddhist preacher. He describes a special kind of spiritual despair that can arise when we block our intrinsic flow of spiritual energy. A person who was proceeding smoothly through life suddenly faces a problem such as illness, hospitalisation, retirement. He was following a path chalked out by his spiritual teacher but suddenly he feels that in spite of practising spiritual disciplines for long years he is not happy. He does not have any peace and has no tangible proof of the inward bliss as has been described by mystics. He wonders what is the use of spending hours in spiritual disciplines or seeking holy company or going to places to listen to discourses on spiritual matters.

In such cases the feeling of hopelessness is inevitable. It is like trying to swim against the current of a swift flowing river. It poses a challenge which can be properly understood only by very few people. They know that this is what the mystics call "the dark night of the soul". Progress is never in a straight line but rather in a wave-like motion. While climbing we have to sometimes go up and at other times go down. Going down apparently means going up in the end.

Spiritual depression and periods of spiritual dryness are thus natural but one should not give up hope. That is the time to assert our real selves and listen to the voice of our inner conscience. There should be a firm conviction that we can overcome such a challenging situation otherwise we are doomed to destruction.

Upto this point we have discussed in great detail the origins of hopelessness, its causes, different phases of hopelessness, and characteristics such as "giving-up-given-up" complex. Now let us talk about something positive to recover hope.

Just as there are many factors which give rise to a feeling of hopelessness, there are equally a number of healthy factors which enable one to establish and maintain strength and a sense of hope which gives us inspiration to take up a positive attitude towards life. In other words, there are factors which instil in us an optimistic attitude if we follow the conditions mentioned below. We shall certainly be able to get rid of hopelessness and make life purposeful. A person who has an optimistic attitude towards life believes that there is a relationship between what he does and what happens—that is, between cause and effect.

In this connection the words of Swami Vivekananda, that we should always have a positive attitude towards life, are important. According to Swamiji we should have faith in ourselves and in the Omnipotent, all powerful Atman in us and all that is good and excellent will come provided we have implicit faith in that. An optimist should think that if he practises what Swamiji said sincerely and wholeheartedly with no negative thinking he will be successful. Once when one of his gurubhais (spiritual brother) was ill, Swamiji wrote in a letter, "Just inject positive thought, Vedantic thought that you have no illness and immediately you will be cured." Autosuggestion is a powerful stimulant for the mind. It gives tremendous strength to overcome feelings of hopelessness.

Therefore the individual with an optimistic frame of mind with hope believes that he has to make an effort to reach the goal. Simply by theorising no result will be achieved. We should imagine that we are at the top of the list of successful candidates in the post graduate examination. But if we just visualise and not work hard, no brilliant result can be expected. Success is not the outcome of wishful thinking. It is the product of both intelligence and industry—*purushakar*. We have to strengthen those ideas which lead to an optimistic frame of mind. Just as hopelessness weakens our energy to respond to a situation, hope strengthens us. We can draw effectively on our energy reservoirs and lead a life that is profoundly inspiring and energising. It gives tremendous energy and has positive effects on our health. Even if we are in a hospital with a serious illness, instead of brooding if we believe in the doctor's assurance that we shall benefit and have faith in the efficacy of the medicine, the healing process gets accelerated.

We can once more quote LeShan who says that an individual should first accept his own being as valid and seek some inner fulfilment. He should believe that life has a meaningful purpose. Even if such a person is a victim of a certain period of helplessness, or temporary set-back, he can overcome it with the belief that human life has meaning and he is destined to do something worthwhile.

Taking this as the core of efforts to overcome hopelessness let us look at some of the steps that a person has to take to get over the feeling of hopelessness. The first point is to get rid of a negative attitude towards life and to revitalise hope through a conscious effort. The conscious mind helps us to gather correct information. In this context the *vijnanamayakosha* which was mentioned earlier must be recalled.

Benefit is immense if we attempt to understand all aspects of a stressful life. A person who has sorrow in life and is suffering from tremendous tension as a result of this has to apply conscious effort and appeal to the *vijnanamayakosha* to get the right guidance and information to tide over the adverse circumstances. That means we have to possess real knowledge, understanding and the capacity to tolerate hardships. In case of accidents such as the death of a beloved person, right understanding helps to lessen the shock whatever its magnitude. If we have no patience to cultivate right understanding, we shall be broken by the blows of fate. When we understand a thing we can bear it more easily.

Let me tell you the story of one brilliant monk of the Ramakrishna Order. It is the tragic case of Swami Atmanandaji, head of the Raipur Centre. Once he was going from Nagpur to Raipur to give a talk on "Vivekachudamani". A brahmachari suggested that since the driver had been driving for a long time he should get some rest. He asked the swami, "If you permit, I shall drive instead of him." The swami was busy preparing for his lecture and absentmindedly agreed to the brahmachari's suggestion. It was raining and the car skidded. It hit a wall and the swami was killed. All the others were thrown out and were safe. It is difficult to say why such things happen. We can only bear them patiently and recover our faith.

Here I am reminded about one of Sri Ramakrishna's sayings recorded in the *Gospel*. There was a monk who was tortured by some people and ultimately killed. While narrating this incident Sri Ramakrishna said that whatever happens does so by the will of God. Some skeptics made a critical comment, "How can tragic accidents happen by the will of God if He is benevolent?" In such instances what we have to do is to reconcile ourselves to fate and think about the law of *karma*.

For instance, we can only see the physical death of a person like Atmanandaji as I described earlier. If Atmanandaji has realised his inner self before his death, his liberation is assured although death occurred under tragic circumstances. That is why the point has to be stressed that understanding the situation does help. When we understand an event hopelessness lessens. Stray incidents then appear as parts of a greater design and we have sufficient knowledge to view them from the right perspective.

The next step to overcome hopelessness is to recover hope through rational thinking. Even people who are grown up often have erroneous, biased ways of interpreting information. In case we want to cultivate a rational frame of mind we should challenge all assumptions. Let me cite an instance: a couple who has been married for long has no children. After a time given the circumstances of the present day world they decide to break the marriage. After the divorce one of them is told that he/she is young and can get married again. The person thinks that he/she has had one bitter experience and is reluctant to take the risk once more. We must challenge this belief by saying that there is no guarantee that a bad experience will be repeated. There may be meaningful love in another attempt. Rational thinking sets negative thoughts right. Inner dialogue and self-analysis are helpful for establishing rational ideas. When we cultivate it, the rigid negative cognitive self weakens and we will be able to have a purposeful attitude towards life.

A concrete example can be cited of a person staying in Bombay whose first marriage failed. He came to me for advice. Afterwards he got married again and has a son. Whenever he comes to Delhi he pays his respects at the temple and then meets me. Obviously, his second marriage is a success. Instead of getting buried under negative thoughts he overcame his difficulty with a rational approach.

A great writer Aaron Beck studied the logic of depressed and discouraged people. Among them he found a number of people with erroneous and faulty thinking.

There can be different categories of this as listed below:

1. Over-generalisation. For example, when we think that once a marriage did not work the second one will go the same way. It is wrong. All cases of divorce are of illogical fallacy.

2. Over-personalising events. If something happens to another person we take it as a personal happening. Often an incident does not produce the required result and judgement is given based on fragments of evidence. Instead we should take a synoptic view which gives a good description of the situation. Magnifying or minimising critical data is also fallacious.

Another important writer Miller coined a term "reality surveillance" as a process helpful in overcoming hopelessness. The meaning of this term is to base our analysis and reasoning on the facts of reality. We should not imagine facts which do not exist. What happens in one case need not be repeated in other similar cases.

But it is often noted that the helpless-hopeless type of people dwell on distant unrealistic goals. If they reach any one of these goals, their will power will be strengthened. The feeling of hopelessness will be lessened. Thus we should aim at goals which are achievable and not those that are impossible. For instance, a late riser makes a resolution to get up early. If he habitually wakes up at 7 a.m., a realistic goal will be to set the time at 6.30 first, then 6, then 5.30. All at once if he wants to get up at 5 it is nearly impossible and will lead to a sense of hopelessness that he is unable to do what he has resolved.

Success breeds success.

Chapter 6

Strength through Will-power

Through the ways mentioned earlier we can recover faith and our will-power is also strengthened. By adopting a positive attitude to life instead of giving in to despair, and getting rid of a pessimistic approach to life are ways of developing *ichha shakti* or will power. This is the real secret of success. None can deny the fact that we want success whatever may be our profession or vocation and the way to achieve success is through the strengthening of will-power.

There are people who are born with some inherent gifts or talents; but even such virtuous people may lack this one important quality, that is will power; in such cases all will come to naught and all will be in vain as the person will not be able to put his gifts to the best possible use. Looking deeply into our own lives we may find that the besetting tragedy of mankind is this lack of will power. Even when we know that something is going to help us we are unable to carry it out because we do not have the necessary tenacity. We are unable to avoid harmful things because our *samskaras* are such that our inborn tendencies prevent us from desisting.

To drive home this point let me use some examples. We all know that we should use pleasant, decent language; that we should not get excited even under the utmost provocation. Psychologists advise that we should keep calm at all times. Somebody abuses me and uses bad language to provoke me but I cannot react. In such a situation we should look inward. A refrain common to everybody is "Many times I got angry and later I regretted it. Let me exercise my will power in future." We know that under trying circumstances we should exercise our will power to the maximum capacity. The formula we have to apply at that moment of extreme anger is: calm down first, try to master your senses, do not give expression to your anger. In this way an awkward situation may be effectively handled. We know that often we get into trouble because we forget to be polite and we lose our temper many times, use bad language and suffer.

We know it is beneficial to lead a moral life. This does not prevent us from committing sinful acts because we cannot help ourselves. For instance, when we go to a temple our mind soars high. We feel elevated. But the moment we do something bad the same mind plunges down. Suppose we watch a video film on the life of Lord Gauranga and witness him lying in samadhi, we are inspired to strive for similar bliss. But when we watch a bad film on the same video, we are doing something we should not. We are aware of our mistake but are unable to stop ourselves. We have no control over ourselves because we lack will power.

In brief, we must have control over our speech, we must desist from sinful acts and strive to do good. But we fail in all these and come to grief. Knowingly and unknowingly we step into this trap of wrong doing. All this is because we are constitutionally weak and sin is the easier way out.

This of course is a negative doctrine. Swami Vivekananda, a true Vedantist, said during one of his lectures in the USA, "Who says we are sinners? It is a sin to call a man a sinner. We are the children of immortal bliss." What he meant was that we are prone to evil not because there is something wrong with us; we are intrinsically pure, divine, a spirit eternally free, according to Swami Vivekananda. We are led to do wrong because we lack will power. Therefore the important point is to strive to cultivate will power without which we will never be able to recover hope.

In effect, we all want to lead a meaningful, purposeful life in this world, to become successful. But we find that in spite of our efforts we fail. The ultimate analysis is that though we have no inherent defect we lack the fundamental virtue of *iccha shakti*. Often I am asked how a person can develop will power. Let me discuss that point now.

Before we discuss the process which leads to the development of will power let us understand what will power is. Will power is that which helps a person to do what he or she knows is good or right and avoid those things which our inner voice tells us is wrong and should not be done under any circumstance.

Will power is something positive and creative which enables us to follow the right path in a definite way. For instance, we would like to get up early in the morning, or not watch a film on video/TV, etc. We decide to remain calm under any provocation. If we develop will power we shall succeed in all this; otherwise we shall fail. Thus we can say that will power is that force which enables us to get rid of all bad forces and helps us to put into practice what we propose to do.

A question which comes to our mind is whether will power can be increased. The answer is, yes. Our past failures should not dishearten us. Let me recount an incident which happened in the life of Saint Augustine, a famous Christian saint who wrote a very valuable book called *Confessions of Saint Augustine*. He suffered from a great conflict. He would make pious resolutions but failed to carry them out due to a weak will power. Everyday he made an attempt and every day he failed. He thought that his was a hopeless case. He would say that for one more day he would lead an immoral life, enjoy the pleasures of the flesh, have a moral holiday and he would reform the

next day. In this way he continued to postpone
his resolution to be good and the prickings of
his conscience made him suffer terrible conflict.

One day he prayed to Jesus and opened a
page in the Bible. The thought came to his mind
that he should not postpone his effort to the next
day, that he should implement it on the same
day. God gave him tremendous strength. He
could turn over a new leaf and recovered his
faith in himself. It was all due to the increase in
his will power. Though Saint Augustine led an
immoral life he had the moral courage to confess
his sins and the ability to rise above them.

Another instance closer to us is that of a
householder disciple of Sri Ramakrishna, Girish
Chandra Ghosh. If we study his life and read
about him in the *Gospel* we find Sri Ramakrishna
blessing Girish wholeheartedly. The reason for
this unique blessing is that Girish had one
virtue among all his numerous vices, and that
was unlimited and unshakeable faith. After
meeting and being influenced by Sri
Ramakrishna he constantly told people about
the tremendous transformation that had taken
place in him. He committed various sins but
never gave up hope. This made it possible for

him to be transformed from an abject sinner to a great saint.

These examples illustrate that we should not be discouraged by past failures. Instead of feeling disheartened we should increase will power so that our past failures need not be our future failures too. What we need to realise is that there should be a determined effort on our part. Like Saint Augustine we should resolve to do today what we would like to postpone for tomorrow. It is never too late to become pure, good and strong.

While discussing the efficacy of developing will power I would like to quote Swami Vivekananda. In soul-stirring words he once said, "Stand up, be bold and strong. Know that you are the creator of your own destiny. All the strength and succour you need is within you." It is a very inspiring message. It tells us in no uncertain terms that we should have tremendous faith in ourselves.

An instance in the life of Swamiji is also worth recalling. About a week before Swamiji passed away, one of his disciples came to him. He was Sarat Chandra Chakrabarty. He was in a very restless frame of mind, and in an agitated

manner he came rushing to his guru at the Belur
Math. The conversation that took place between
them has been recorded in a book called *Swami
Shisya Sambad*. We are told that in spite of being
initiated by Swamiji, Sarat Chandra failed to
meditate properly. He lacked the will power to
concentrate his mind. That day he had made up
his mind to ask his guru for a solution to this
problem. He was worried that in spite of having
such an exceptional guru, the most illustrous
disciple of Sri Ramakrishna, he was a failure in
inward life.

Vivekananda could fathom what was in his
disciple's mind. That day Swamiji was taking a
walk on the bank of the Ganga. In those days
there was no big temple dedicated to Sri
Ramakrishna or Holy Mother at Belur Math.
There was only Vivekananda's quarters,
monastery and kitchen. In such a place when
Swamiji was walking, his disciple approached
him with his problem. As soon as Sarat Chandra
saluted Swamiji, the latter knew the reason for
this visit and told him not to say anything at that
time. Instead Swamiji asked his beloved disciple
to meet him in his room after the evening arati.
They would then be alone and could find a

solution to the problem in peace.

Naturally the disciple was overjoyed to get this assurance from his guru. He would get an opportunity to have his guru absolutely to himself which is a rare privilege for a disciple. Sarat Chandra then went to the old temple and attended the arati. After that he silently went to Swamiji's room and found his guru absorbed in deep meditation. He thought that it was a great privilege to see Swamiji in such a state. He should not unload his mind or disturb his guru at such a moment. Silently he took his position in one corner of the room and sat observing Swamiji. After some time Vivekananda opened his eyes and looked very compassionately at his beloved disciple. He wanted to give his disciple an opportunity to serve him. He asked for a glass of water. The disciple was happy to do this small service for the guru. Then he thought he would get the chance to put his question to Swamiji. Before he could put his thoughts into words Swamiji himself said, "My son, today I had deep meditation." That was Sarat Chakrabarty's question too! He said, "Maharaj, I have come with that same question. You are my guru and you have given me the *maha mantra*. In spite of that, however much I try I find that my limitations and shortcomings surface and I fail miserably to meditate. Will this rare human birth go in vain? I have taken refuge in you. You had deep concentration of mind today. Will you please bless me in such a way that I too can have that kind of concentration whenever I sit for meditation? My mind is so wild that it always goes in different directions. Please help me to get some success in meditation." Swamiji heard him and said, "Well, you are my beloved disciple and I assure you that you will have success. But you are very young and young people are generally impatient. You must wait and you will get everything in the fullness of time."

The disciple was anxious to get an immediate, ready-made solution to his problem. He said that he could not bear to wait for an indefinite period. He wanted to hear the magic words from the lips of his guru that very evening. Swamiji had the maturity of a true teacher and did not get excited. He rose to the occasion and said, "In the course of time even a tiny little creature crawling on the floor will be liberated and you, who are my disciple, won't you also be liberated? Certainly you will have concentration and everything else you want. But my son, you must remember four things." And the four instructions Swamiji gave his disciple were "be possessed of strength, be possessed of faith, attain to knowledge of your own divine self and dedicate yourself for the good of humanity."

This incident is extremely relevant to our problem because the four points Swamiji spoke about to his disciple are also necessary for us to cultivate. Swamiji said, "Have faith in yourself. Be bold, be strong, have this faith that you are the creator of your destiny. All the power and strength you need is within yourself." If we love Swamiji, if we have faith in our great cultural heritage, we must have this tremendous faith. We should believe that we have infinite possibilities within us. If we are prone to commit mistakes because of our lower animal or biological nature, we must remember that we also have something divine in us. We should try our best to manifest this divinity within us. We should assert our higher self and be always conscious of the elevated dimensions of life. This is possible only when we cultivate *shraddha, atma shraddha*. Tremendous self-confidence is what this implies—self-confidence that goes a long way in recovering faith. It helps us in no mean measure to develop our will-power which we have seen is the pivot of all achievements in life.

This point may appear slightly paradoxical. We have to have firm faith to develop will-power and in its turn will-power gives us firm faith. We have to be conscious of our divine heritage and believe that we have unlimited power within. We have to tap the source of power within and cultivate the attitude that we are not tiny little creatures breaking down at the smallest provocation. We are the children of immortal bliss. All power is invested in us. Once we come to have this faith we will be able to manifest, in the real sense of the term, tremendous power that is inside us. Thereby we will be successful in developing will-power.

Of course, all this follows only if we develop will-power with the help of Swamiji's assurance: "You are the children of immortal bliss. Who says you are sinners? Forget about your past mistakes." The next step is to develop love for our intrinsic divine nature. The more love we develop towards the truth of our real being, the more will we succeed in developing will power or *ichha shakti*.

A question may be asked whether it is

possible to develop will-power overnight? The answer is "No". We may have to pass through long periods of tremendous struggle. No success is possible without working hard for it and there is no joy in achieving success without effort. We must, therefore, prepare for a tremendous struggle. We may not succeed overnight but ultimately victory is assured.

Here we have to take one thing into consideration. Once we are inspired by Swamiji's words and we develop love for the truth of our inner divinity, then we should resolve that no hypothetical fear be allowed to sabotage our self-confidence or inner energy. We should keep the memory of Swamiji's words constantly in our mind that we are not sinners, that we are the children of immortal bliss. It is true that in our weaker moments we may feel that we have limitations and that life is only an unending process of abject misery. This negative attitude often plagues us. But when our will-power is well developed we have the courage and conviction to change the direction of such negative impulses. Swamiji told us that in such moments of weakness we should assert our higher self and fight against the evil forces. The constant tug of war between the evil forces of our lower self and the power of our higher self is an exercise in cultivating strength and conviction.

Swamiji once said, "Since death is inevitable, let life go after a noble conquest." We should fight for the conquest of the evil forces which cause despair and despondency, which plague us with negative thoughts. We feel that our limitations hinder us from strengthening our will power. But under such conditions we should keep in mind Swamiji's challenging words, "Have you got the will to surmount the mountain high obstructions? Even if the whole world stands against you, would you still dare to do what is right?"

Before concluding let us recollect that the important point here is *shraddha*. There are two fundamental obstacles to the cultivation of will power: exaggerated regret about the past and excessive worrying about the future. We should not worry too much about what the future has in store for us, nor should we regret overmuch the acts we have done in the past. As a poet said,

"Let the dead past bury its dead!
Act, act, in the living present,
Trust no future, however pleasant."

Let us, therefore, act in the living present. The present cannot be properly utilised if we are brooding over the past or anticipating the future with anxiety. To develop will power it is essential that we lead a very alert life, in the living present.

Here we are reminded of a great German mystic, Eckhart who said, "In the heart of this moment is eternity." If you want to enjoy eternal life, if you want to hold communion with the Eternal, then remember that you have to live well and do your best in the present.

Let us avoid living in the past or the future; let us learn to live in the present and make proper use of it. If we can do that, then it will help us immensely to develop will power and bring the right balance into life. In turn this helps overcome all kinds of mental tension. In a word, living in the present is an effective cure for mental troubles.

Chapter 7

Infinite Possibilities of the Inner Self

In the previous pages some aspects of will power have been identified. Now we have to analyse certain factors that are detrimental to the cultivation of will power. One has been mentioned already, that is, preoccupation with past or future and neglect of the present. Such an obsession will damage our present, weaken our minds and considerably injure our future. Therefore, we should spare no pains to lead a wakeful life in the living present.

Our great rishis have told us to have faith in the infinite possibilities of our inner self. The truth is that we are spirits eternally free—birthless and deathless. The trouble arises when we forget the higher dimension of life and identify ourselves with the limitations of the body and mind. We then descend to a lower plane, attach reality merely to the body and the mind and suffer as a result.

As against this, in moments of depression, nervous tension and weakness, if we can remember our higher self, the divine spark, then from the point of view of the Atman we have no further problem. Instead of making much of the so-called weaknesses and limitations of our mind and body we should have tremendous faith in our own Atman. Swami Vivekananda in one place said that if we believe we are Atman, power will come, purity will come, all that is good will come. Once we are roused to the realisation of our real Self, once we are rooted in this Self, we shall see how our will-power grows.

Therefore the secret of developing will-power is through having faith in the real dimension of life. We may be frail from the point of view of the body and mind but from the real standpoint we are nothing other than Brahman. As Sankaracharya rightly said, *Jeeva brahmanviyo na paro*. We should call upon our mind again and again to increase our will-power because it goes a long way in overcoming mental tension.

Sometimes parents complain that the present generation of children are disobedient. My reply to such people is that we have to first bring ourselves up properly before we can bring up our children. Unless we can manifest the infinite potential within us and train our mind by subjecting it to some kind of mental discipline, we shall not be complete human beings. When we have achieved this standard, then alone can we think of correcting the ways of the younger generation.

There may be a number of factors likely to sabotage our efforts to cultivate will-power. For example, a person decides, "I will turn over a new leaf. I will be regular in my visits to the Mission. I will go to listen to the religious discourses regularly. I must lead a purposeful, meaningful life.If I just waste my valuable life in running after frivolous things of the world, then this whole life will go in vain." Some people may proceed in this direction but such persons may come across people who thoughtlessly ridicule them by saying, "Why do you waste a Sunday evening in such a foolish manner? You should go to the club or watch television. Why go to the Mission?" Such criticism is difficult to bear.

There may also be selfish people. Suppose a person decides to lead a life of righteousness. He makes a vow, "I shall earn money by honest and sincere means. I will not stoop low to earn money. I will not adopt any corrupt means." We are surrounded by corrupt people who are always trying to lead us astray. Such people may even torment us and insist that we do wrong instead of setting an example of honesty. Under such pressure a person may deteriorate.

Our friends may regard our behaviour as strange. Often people tell me that if they resolve to devote their time in meaningful pursuits their friends tell them that since they are so young they should be enjoying life instead of thinking about serious or religious concerns.

These are some of the circumstances where one must renew one's efforts towards the cultivation of will-power. When such situations arise because of the critical attitude of people we care for, we should become all the more alert.

Further, we must chalk out a certain routine to help us develop will-power. A life led in a desultory fashion cannot help us in this path. Suppose we get up at 5 a.m. one day and at 7 a.m. the next day, if we do not have fixed time for food, relaxation, and other habitual activity, we can never have strong will- power. If we look into the lives of great people, we find that they scrupulously follow a typical routine.

Let me tell you about my student days. As a student of philosophy one day I visited a bookshop in Calcutta after finishing my M.A. classes. There I found a book on *The lives of Great Philosophers of the World*. Immediately I bought a copy of the book. It was the year 1949 and I was not a monk then. I read with engrossing interest the lives of all the important philosophers. While reading about Immanuel Kant I discovered that his life was so ordered he had a fixed time even for taking the morning walk. People would set their watches with his movements!

We must also subject ourselves to some kind of strict routine. Of course, there may be some instances where we can slacken the time-table but by and large we should try to keep to the routine. This should be drawn up after proper deliberation and adhered to carefully. To develop will-power self-improvement must be effected at all levels —physical, mental and spiritual.

The next point to remember is that we need great power of concentration in order to develop will-power. In fact here is a circular route because will-power helps the growth of the power of concentration and the power of concentration in turn helps will-power to increase.

Power of concentration can be developed while performing ordinary tasks everyday. For instance, if we are asked to arrange flower vases, this can be done in a half-hearted manner when the mind is not fully devoted to the work we are performing. When the mind roams here and there while doing work ,we should know that we lack concentration. The attitude we should cultivate is that the work we are doing is our duty, it is our worship. Even while arranging flowers we must do it meticulously. If we are polishing our shoes or attending to a patient in our clinic, we should work with full concentration and give our entire attention to work in hand. A mother working in the kitchen can also do her work with full concentration. Any kind of job can be done in this way and when the whole mind is devoted to the job, gradually it will help our power of concentration to improve and also make our will-power strong.

Another important point for cultivating will power is that we must have sufficient reserve of mental energy. Generally our mental energy is limited and we often fritter it away in idle conversation, purposeless work, futile controversies, back-biting, day dreaming, sinful or lurid thoughts, concern for unnecessary things, hypothetical fears. All these are detrimental to the development of will-power. First we should analyse how much of our valuable time and precious mental energy is wasted in speaking ill of others, useless criticism and such activities. We should view the whole problem with the attitude that we have got this rare human birth through the grace of God; we should make something out of it. We should lead a purposeful life as there is much to do in this limited time. If we are whole-heartedly engaged in the task of our own self-improvement, we will have no time to find fault with others. This will conserve our mental energy and channelise it in the right direction to make our will-power invincible. Holy Mother Sri Sarada Devi said, "If you want peace of mind, do not find fault with others." We can analyse our own faults instead. The world will be a Heaven if we can remember this simple instruction of the Holy Mother. Even our Brahmacharis who take this vow often forget it and criticise others. They deviate from the path shown by Holy Mother. In such cases the solution is to pray to God saying that we have broken a vow and we should be forgiven. In future we should be helped to keep our vow. Failure in one instance should not seriously affect our progress. It is said that repeated failures are the surest path to success. We should not lose heart. Failure is a part of the game of life.

In connection with the need to avoid useless discussion I am reminded of one important verse from the *Vivekachudamani*. In verse no. 367 we are told: *Yogasya prathamam dwaram vak nirodha*: if we want to enter the state of yoga the first gate is the control of speech. Speech here does not mean merely the act of speaking but also all the organs of action.

A direct disciple of Sri Ramakrishna, Swami Turiyananda, had written spiritual instructions in the form of letters in Bengali which have subsequently been translated under the title *Spiritual Treasures*. In one of the letters Turiyanandaji confessed that he had a habit of talking excessively. Then he came across the verse of Sankaracharya which I have already quoted above. It made him realise how much mental energy he was wasting in unnecessary words and useless discussions. He realised that he should have absolute control over his speech.

It is a common observation that men of powerful will are also men of few words. They live with a purpose and their ideal is to talk less. They are active and dynamic, nor merely visionary. They live a life which is intense, not tense! And there is a world of difference between being intense and being tense. One way of avoiding mental tension is to exercise control over speech for it gives us energy to devote to other aspects of life. A person who is in the habit of speaking constantly feels exhausted after a certain period of time. That is why the monks often observe a vow of silence for long periods. Periodically Mahatma Gandhi used to observe silence.

I knew a Swamiji, a knower of the Brahman, who used to hear the *anahata dhvani*. He was the disciple of Holy Mother Sri Sarada Devi. His name was Swami Shantananda. In 1951 when he was in the T.B. Sanitorium in Ranchi I had the good fortune of coming into contact with him. At least once a week he would observe silence for a day and he himself told me that he heard *omkar dhvani*. In his early life he spent much time in singing hymns and devotion in Varanasi. He had observed silence for many months at a time in his early life. When he was observing the vow, a woman disciple of Sri Ramakrishna, Yogen Ma came to Varanasi. She heard about the great austerity of Swami Shantanandaji and went to meet him. He came out of his room to see her but could not speak because of his vow of silence. After some time Yogen Ma went away.

Later Shantanandaji's conscience troubled him. He wondered whether he had done the right thing in keeping his vow. Yogen Ma was no ordinary woman. She was the disciple of the Master, the constant companion of the Holy Mother and a highly respected person among the Ramakrishna Order. When his period of silence was over he happened to meet a senior monk Swami Turiyanandaji in Varanasi and asked him, "Maharaj, perhaps I made a mistake in not breaking my vow of silence when Yogen Ma came to meet me."

Swami Turiyanandaji was like a lion in strength and conviction. He said, "Take courage, you did not do anything wrong. You were absolutely right. Don't try to please anybody except God." To him the vow of silence was more important than observance of social niceties.

Another instance of the power of silence is

in the life of my own guruji, Swami Virajanandaji. He has to his credit a very valuable book, *Paramartha Prasanga* or *Towards the Goal Supreme*. He describes how once he felt no zeal for work after the passing away of Swami Vivekananda in 1902. In those days he was busy campaigning for the *Prabuddha Bharata*. He told his brother disciple Swarupanandaji, the then President of the Advaita Ashrama to give him leave so that he could devote time to prayer and meditation. Then he took a vow of silence. In his autobiography, *Atiter Smriti* or *Story of an Epoch* it is mentioned that he continued to observe silence for about one and a half years continuously. In this way he recouped his lost zeal.

A vow of silence thus gives us tremendous energy. Of course, for householders continuous silence is impossible at home or in the work environment. But we can do it in another way by avoiding unnecessary words. That itself will also serve to a great extent as a vow of silence.

Another way of conserving energy is to lead a pure life. If our minds are weak and shallow and impure, we shall have no will power. The great individuals whom the world has seen have all said that by conserving energy in this manner we can develop will power. Apart from mental energy which we saw can be conserved by talking less, we should also make an effort to conserve our physical energy, especially sexual energy. This needs a lot of care. Those who thoughtlessly and deliberately squander away their valuable physical energy are bound to have shallow minds. That is why our ancient rishis have taught us: *Ojo oshi*: Oh God, you are full of *ojos*, grant us this *ojos*. You are full of virility and strength, give us this strength.

Much, therefore, depends on purity and we should make an effort to lead a pure life. Swami Vivekananda warned us that all things that make us weak physically, intellectually or morally should be avoided like poison. We should practise purity in thought, word and deed. Again in this, for householders absolute continence may not be possible; even then we have to be careful and try to preserve our physical energy as much as we can.

Further, to develop will power we should not indulge in negative thinking. Failure often makes us take a gloomy view of life and we stop making any effort to bring ourselves back on the right track. If we analyse our failures we shall become aware that they are the result of faulty thoughts. Suppose we give in to temptation easily—as for instance, going to the club instead of coming to the Mission to hear a talk on "How to Overcome Mental Tension" the wrong thought is translated into action. Such thought lead us astray while right thought lead us to a larger good. Therefore, we can strengthen our will power only when we keep a rein over our thoughts and prevent wrong thoughts from being translated into action.

At this point it may be asked how thoughts can be given the right direction. It is often seen that in spite of pious resolutions to avoid evil and do good a moment of weakness spoils the resolution. A friend comes and motivates us in the wrong way and we succumb to this powerful motivation. The way to prevent thoughts from going in the wrong direction is by controlling that weakness which instigates us to do certain things. Sometimes in spite of being aware of our mistake we are unable to prevent it. Then the conflict is very painful.

In this connection I am reminded of Buddha's instruction to some monks. In his search for the meaning of existence these *bikshus* had left home and renounced the world. In spite of that they had difficulties from their own mind. Buddha told them, "Remember, O *bikshus*, the only way to become victorious over wrong thoughts is to review from time to time the phases of one's own mind, to reflect upon them, to root out all that is evil and cultivate all that is good." This is a very powerful process of self-improvement.

Therefore, will power is necessary to be victorious over wrong thoughts and they in turn will strengthen our will power. In conclusion, let me summarise that we must possess purity of intention and purity of conduct to succeed in life. If we are convinced about the efficacy of Swamiji's words that we should reject as poison whatever degrades us, we shall be able to control our minds and bodies effectively. We should pray to Tathagatha that his instruction to the *bikshus* to root out all that is evil should become possible in our lives too. We should implore him to come to our rescue, give us the necessary strength to get over our lapses and become established in good by strengthening our will power. We should ask him to make us real men and women of character.

Chapter 8

Need for Prayer to Control Mental Tension

Sometimes, in spite of our sincere efforts to be good we fail because of our limitations. In such a situation our most essential task is to pray sincerely to the God in us for strength and succour.

In this connection let me mention *The Gospel of Sri Ramakrishna*. In it Sri Ramakrishna repeats constantly that God-realisation is the only goal of human life. When we pray to God we should pray for *shuddha bhakti*, he said. That is, pure devotion for his lotus feet. While laying stress on the efficacy of prayer the Master also made it imperative that while praying for pure devotion we should ask God to make our will power strong. We should plead with God to give us tremendous *ichha shakti* so that we are in a position to do what is right and desist from what is wrong. If we are conscious of our limitations which make us weak and fail in whatever we undertake, we should pray that we can overcome these obstacles with the help of sufficient will power.

We must remember that prayer does produce result provided it is sincere. It has been said that nothing in this world can be attained by mere prayer. What we can do is to pray continuously and repeat the Lord's name incessantly so that it helps us to develop will power which in turn will help us achieve remarkable results in all that we do. We are unable to develop will power due to the impurities of our mind. When we are engaged in constant prayer, these blemishes slowly dissolve and our minds are purified. As Buddha advised, we shall then be in a position to identify and root out all that is evil in our minds and gain mental strength.

In addition to prayer, we should control the desire to blame ourselves constantly for our faults. As Swami Virajanandaji, the sixth President of the Ramakrishna Order said in the book already mentioned, that is *Towards the Goal Supreme*, we should not go on talking about our own defects because this makes us lose our self-respect. If we are conscious of our flaws, let us confess to the Lord and pray to Him for strength to overcome them.

In other words, the primary need is to surrender ourselves completely to the will of God. We should tell Him how utterly helpless we feel and how much we desire Him to come to our rescue. Our acknowledgement of our own helplessness brings us to an attitude of self-surrender. This is the right position in which God comes to us and gives us the necessary courage to avoid doing evil.

Here we can remember what Lord Jesus said in one place, "Without me you can do nothing."

Bhagawan Sri Krishna in the eighteenth chapter of the Gita also said something similar to Arjuna, "If you fail, you should have an attitude of whole-hearted surrender to Me. Take refuge in Me, take shelter in Me, then I will do everything for you."

Thus, to overcome the feeling of hopelessness and thereby get rid of mental tension we have to practise self-analysis and introspection. From time to time we should take recourse to inner dialogue which is also a form of prayer. True self-confrontation is a process of recovering hope. It will reveal to us the purpose of life.

The purpose of life is of two broad categories: a relative purpose and an ultimate purpose. Worldly success falls into the first category as for instance, excellence in a particular profession. Then the question arises as to whether we have any absolute aim in life. The desire to become conscious of our real nature constitutes our absolute purpose. Realisation of the higher dimension of life, beyond the finite self with its limitations and imperfections gives us tremendous strength and shows us that there is something divine in us.

When we come face to face with our own self during rigorous analysis and in-depth introspection we are plagued by questions about the meaning and purpose of existence. For instance, as a computer engineer a person earns fifty thousand rupees and his aim is to earn more and more. This becomes a relative goal and ultimately this cannot continue to make us happy. Even after amassing lakhs of rupees we do not know how to train the mind and then we are a prey to mental tensions. The solution is to probe deeply into our inner reality. We should aim at realising the extremely significant inward self within us.

The first task is to differentiate between the relative and the absolute goals in our life. Then we should take steps to achieve that which we want by delineating action and proceeding towards the goal we set before us. Simply imagining it will not do. Suppose we want to visit the holy Amarnath cave, unless we take a pony we have to walk a long way. We have to proceed step by step to reach our destination. Waiting at Pahalgaun and saying we have reached Amarnath in our imagination will never take us there. From Pahalgaun we have to go to Chandanbari and then to Amarnath. Just by imagining we have gone there is not enough. We have to be practical.

Sri Ramakrishna gives an example in the *Gospel* about how to realise God. He says that a person is told that there is valuable treasure buried in a place. Just standing at that spot and thinking about the treasure will not make the person rich. He has to make an effort to dig the ground, work hard at it in order to reach the treasure. We can thus proceed slowly towards the goal instead of attaining it in a moment through imagination.

Since introspection is an important step in

the direction of efficacious prayer let us see how we can best carry it out. For introspection we require a period of solitude. Introspection is not easy. While we are analysing ourselves we may find the causes of our mental tension. We may then minimise or suppress these causes and say there is nothing to worry about in such minor faults. In this way we silence the voice of our conscience.

The remedy to this is to go into solitude from time to time and look carefully at the workings of our own mind, as Buddha advises. In the beginning this may involve much serious struggle. But slowly we shall be able to ferret out those aspects of our mind which are hiding from us and realise our own self better.

Once we succeed in some amount of self-analysis the next step is a kind of healthy self-acceptance. Each person has his own desires and inhibitions and realising these defects makes him careful to avoid them in future. Self-affirmation is also an acceptance of our own limitations. We come face to face with the emotional aspects of our desires and learn to confront them. From this follows the next step which is called self-integration. We learn about ourselves and try to successfully integrate all these into a balanced personality. In that state even if someone criticises us we do not react immediately. We have the maturity to think that perhaps such criticism is for our own good.

Often people say that they have difficulty in controlling their temper. They also say that later they regret their outburst but on the spur of the moment if someone gives them advice about how to control themselves they get angrier and shout, "Who are you to give me advice?" But those who have undergone self-analysis and self-integration will not react in such violent manner. They will be able to think that the other person is possibly giving sound advice. It should be taken in the right spirit and through interpreting such criticism in a heathy manner we help ourselves to grow.

Also, as a result of self-integration our personality loses its self-centredness. Some of us are extremely self-centred. We become so selfish that we look only to our own interest. One way to overcome mental tension is to think of others and work for the welfare of others. We can do so provided we practise introspection. Introspection leads to self-integration; it cures us of selfish motives and gives us impetus to work for others.

We can take the example of the numerous people who come to the Ramakrishna Mission to offer us voluntary service. Often people come to us the very next day of their retirement from service and say, "Please give us some work." Their motive is not to earn money. They have developed a broader outlook. They feel that for sixty years they have served their family, relatives and friends. Now they would like to do something for the welfare of others. They acquire this spirit of service through self-analysis. For the same reason people spend time in looking after plants and animals. These activities have a therapeutic effect in overcoming mental tension. Such things make life acquire meaning.

Another method which helps us to recover hope and cures us of mental stress is taking a real view of the world, different from the narrow one which we usually have. The ordinary view of the world is grossly materialistic—to amass wealth, enjoy life since it is assumed that there is nothing beyond the world. Those who suffer from mental tension or hopelessness are steeped in this materialistic life and know nothing beyond its cause and effect. Such people do not care for self-analysis and self-confrontation. As against this are the people who are able to look beyond the material facade of the world and adopt a real view which helps them to rise above mental strain. They take recourse to self-analysis and introspection. They cultivate a positive way of thinking and believe that each one of their actions has a positive effect.

When a person is suffering from a serious illness and everything looks dismal, he becomes a victim of different kinds of hopeless, negative feelings. One wonders why such trials come. But we should remember that out of evil comes good. Every experience has a positive aspect. Suffering gives an opportunity for personal, spiritual growth. The only thing is we should be able to alter our attitude to life in times of adversity.

In this connection let us take two concrete examples. Swami Vivekananda was a genius and a world mover, an incarnation of Siva, so to say. He has many achievements to his credit and was introduced by Professor Wright of the Harvard University at the Parliament of

Religions with these words: "Here is a person more learned than all our learned men put together." A person of such exceptional talents as Swamiji could not get a job when his family was facing abject poverty! When we read about this phase in his biography tears come to our eyes unbidden. Young Naren went from place to place frantically but there was no job to be had. He was therefore filled with doubt about the very existence of God. His father had died unexpectedly and his family was in acute financial crisis. Sometimes there was no rice to feed the entire family. Swamiji would pretend to his mother that he had eaten with a friend so that his share could be given to the others. Everyday he would leave the house taking the name of the Lord, and look for a job. His mother scolded him saying what was the use of taking the name of the Lord who seemed deaf to their entreaties. That is how Swamiji also lost his faith momentarily and shouted at a person who was singing the glories of God to stop such nonsense. From this difficult period of his life Swamiji learnt to feel for the poor in India. Without this experience he would not have been able to identify himself with the millions of suffering in his motherland. That is why he could say, "Put off meditation till the next life. I don't believe in any other God. My God is the poor, the wicked. Know that service to them is the highest religion. May I be born again and again to serve these people." Vivekananda could give the right direction to people and relieve humankind of suffering because he himself had suffered immensely.

The other person is St. Teresa. She too was a world mover. She was admitted to a convent school. Due to her beauty and amiability other nuns had an eye on her becuse they thought she would make a good nun. They constantly asked her when she would accept the vows of a nun. She would reply that her parents had sent her there for education and she had no intention of becoming a nun. But God had His own design for her. Once Teresa fell terribly ill and was reduced to a skeleton. After that she looked at her body which had been so very beautiful earlier and wondered at the transitory nature of the body. She realised that beauty was perishable. She questioned herself, "Is there anything in me that is imperishable?" She came to understand the truth of the nuns' wish that she should join their order. She came to feel that Jesus was the only reality. She thought, "If this body is perishable, let the body be crucified so that the spirit in me can be resurrected." The period of her suffering had roused in her the dormant divinity. She joined the convent as a nun, started her own organisation and became a name in the world of mysticism.

Therefore there is truth in Swamiji's words that out of misfortune comes good. We can verify this in our own life and cultivate a spiritual attitude to replace the grossly materialistic one. Suffering is inevitable on the path of spiritual unfoldment. We have to realise that the entire life is a manifestation of supreme eternal consciousness. We must try to look within and discover our inner self. This is a source of immense joy and as soon as we discover it, our life is changed. In this attitude a person becomes immersed in spirituality. Then there is no place for mental tension. Spiritual strength gives us courage to cope with stress and to overcome it. Therefore, the solution to our conflict and confusion is developing a spiritual attitude to life.

Chapter 9

Impact of Meditation on Mental States

As we have discussed already, one of the best ways of overcoming mental tension is to practise regular meditation. It is a tried and tested technique. While practising meditation it is not necessary for us to be wedded to any particular philosophy. Even an agnostic, or an atheist can practise meditation. It is a tool which can be used to rise above emotional stress and overcome mental tension. Each of us should therefore earmark a certain amount of time each day for practising meditation. This would mean we should spend the time quietly in self-analysis, introspection and other such inward directed activities mentioned earlier.

In order to stress the efficacy of meditation, let us take a place like Delhi which is the capital of India. Here we can hardly find any solitary place where we can retire to hold communion with our inner nature. Many devotees say, "Swamiji, if you ask to practise meditation we have to go either to the Himalayas or to places like Shimla, Almora, or Mayavati, where nature is serene with the majestic Himalayas in the background. In such surroundings even a person who is not inclined to meditation is forced to do so. But what about Delhi? Is it possible to meditate here?" My reply to this is an affirmative: yes. It is possible to meditate even under these circumstances.

We have to remember that it is not possible for all of us to retire to an isolated place of retreat. We have our everyday activities. Living in a place which is crowded, in a society within which we have to function and fulfil all our obligations we still have to strive to maintain mental balance by training our mind rigorously.

When I mention the effort to acquire mental balance, I would like to remind you that we are the citizens of two worlds. The average individual will tell me that we are the citizens of free India. But we must not forget that this is only a part of our existence. We have two levels at which we function, the external and internal realities. Even those people who are unaware of their inner being are well able to relate to the external reality and make the best of all it has to offer. Now in our effort to overcome mental tension we have to make a conscious effort to bridge the gap between this and the other world, that is, the world of inner reality.

Our experience in the world teaches us that there is tremendous pressure from the external world. Any field of activity that we choose, whether as a teacher, a doctor, an advocate, or an administrator puts a huge amount of pressure on us. Under this pressure we often lose control over ourselves and then an integrated life becomes impossible. We may want to lead a balanced life but the socio-economic pressures create many disturbances and we lose our mental balance. We therefore need some technique that will bridge the gap between our external disturbances and inner dimension in order to maintain a tranquil frame of mind.

And that technique is called meditation. It is a practical, systematic method which enables us and teaches us to control inner conflicts to obtain peace of mind. Taking recourse to meditation from time to time helps us to meet the challenges of the external world instead of running away from them. We are not talking about the total absorption of mystics who retire permanently into the solitude of the Himalayas and get immersed in meditation. For them it is easy to be engrossed in meditation. Also, we cannot agree with the dictum that only by going to secluded places we can meditate. We can meditate anywhere as long as we have trained our minds properly. Otherwise even in the Himalayas we may fail to practise intense meditation.

Wherever we go the mind goes with us. The aim is to learn to keep it under control. Then we shall be able to maintain its tranquility even in the midst of our extremely busy schedule. To train the mind properly and learn the true technique of meditation, we have to face our experiences and not run away from them. We can live in the world and enjoy ourselves well without being affected by the rush and stress of the modern world. We have to learn to perform our tasks diligently and yet be above the stress and strain of emotional conflicts or of excessive involvement.

This is possible when we know how to practise meditation in action. Clinical experiments have proved that one of the main causes of emotional disturbances and mental tension is the ignorance about our own self. The result is that we are born, we grow up, develop, decay and die and this rare human birth goes in vain. We never become conscious of the reality in us, the self in us, the Atman in us. Life becomes fulfilling and meaningful only when we are able to comprehend our true divine nature.

From the beginning of our life we are not trained to discover our inner self. As we grow up we have consciousness only of our apparent self. We never explore the possibility of discovering real happiness away from the mundane, external objects into a dimension that is within us. Once we are aware of the futility and transitoriness of externals, we turn our gaze inwards and through meditation we try to reach that real peace and contentment that lie hidden.

We have to therefore pause and ponder for a few minutes each day to get charged with spiritual energy. This is meditation. It equips us to face any challenge and win. If we focus too much of attention on the material goals of life, we are dragged away from the inner reality. If we are always obsessed with the external world, the material comforts and the outward dimension of life, it will be very difficult for us to overcome mental tension.

However much we enjoy all that the world has to offer, we cannot avoid a sense of fear, uncertainty and depression. These can be cured only with the help of meditation. Through meditation alone we can discover our real self which is the source of tremendous strength.

Swami Vivekananda used to say that everyone should be taught about their divine nature. Once we have roused our divine nature, we shall be able to tap the strength hidden there. This becomes possible when we practise meditation.

The practice of meditation has been taught in all the major religions of the world. Even Christian and Sufi mystics speak about it. Our Eastern methods of meditation, especially Patanjali's Yoga Sutras, serve as models of meditation.

We should first realise that meditation is not only for the sadhus who have taken *diksha*. Any person, whether initiated or not, can practise meditation as it benefits mental health. It is as useful to an executive as it is to a plumber or a student, teacher, housewife. Meditation is a tool that can benefit everyone. Those who practise meditation daily will corroborate my statement. The day we succeed in meditating well is the day we become free from all kinds of tensions. There is ample factual evidence to support its truth.

Christian mystics have described how in the face of challenging situations they sit in their room and practise intense meditation. They hold communion with their inner nature. Then they are well equipped to face the problems. It is true that all power, all strength is hidden within us and we have to know how to tap the source. If we live on the surface without diving deep, and meet provocations in this mental frame, we will often be upset. But if we are firmly established in the glory of the Atman we can meet any situation without getting ruffled. Therefore, meditation is absolutely essential.

To learn and practise meditation we have to take the help of a teacher. Swami Vivekananda said in his lecture on Raja Yoga that a person who practises the technique outlined by him is sure to benefit since it is a proven method. He has given many hints in that lecture about how to practise meditation. Learning this from a competent teacher helps to avoid mistakes, overcome pitfalls, and ultimately be self-reliant to make the journey alone. A guru gives us instructions on how to get mental peace by meditating. But it is no use just listening to such teaching. No benefit comes unless we practise what we are taught. To strengthen our mental make-up we must therefore practise meditation in all seriousness as it helps to correct our erroneous attitudes towards life and the world.

As was already mentioned, meditation is an on-going process of self-discovery and self-integration. Through meditation we discover the Reality in us and then lead an integrated life. Our energies are collected and channelled in a positive direction instead of being frittered away in many useless directions. Meditation helps to quieten the racing mind and give us the right attitude to seek our true self.

In guided meditation we are taught to focus our attention on the sanctuary of the heart, imagining the presence of our beloved deity there. If we are to take the method of jnanis we follow the path of discrimination. Then we are told to focus on the inner self. The consciousness of the presence of the inner reality in us calms our minds, soothes our nerves and brings a feeling of immense inner peace. Regular meditation enables us to get rid of negative influences. Sometimes we are weighed down by negative thoughts, brood about wrong things and indulge in weakening ideas. To transform them into positive paths the only method is to practise meditation.

In the history of meditation we are told about the stages which lead to the final concentration. Patanjali's yoga speaks about *pratyahara, dharana, dhyana* and finally *samadhi*. Before we discuss these, let me remind you that the essential aspect of the practice of meditation is to take good care of our physical health. If we have a weak constitution, we may fail in meditation. We should therefore do regular physical exercises including pranayam or breathing exercises. A sound mind and a sound body are two aspects which go together and neither should be neglected.

Let us now see what Swami Vivekananda has to say about controlling the mind. Before we can hope to be successful in meditation we should be aware of the restless nature of the mind. While speaking in the West Swamiji spoke of the restless mind by comparing it to a monkey. Then, under the influence of an intoxicant such as wine it becomes more wild. When stung by a scorpion it becomes almost impossible to control the monkey.

Such is the nature of our minds. Swamiji repeated again and again the difficulties of controlling such a mind. He used metaphors to describe the stages of increasing restlessness in the monkey: when a demon enters it, when he is stung, or has drunk wine. All these find similarities with the human mind. It becomes drunk with the wine of desire, is stung by the scorpion of jealousy, and finally the demon of pride enters the mind making it think of itself as all-important. In this way he cautions us about how hard it is to control the mind.

Arjuna put a question on the same topic to Krishna in the battlefield of Kurukshetra. Sri Krishna admitted that it is very difficult to control the mind. It is turbulent and the senses are running in different directions. He suggested that *abhyas* and *vairagya*—detachment and discrimination between the real and unreal— are paths to follow.

Likewise, Swamiji, after using the analogy of the monkey for the restless mind suggests some remedies. He says, "The first lesson is to sit quietly for some time and let the mind run on."

Our lives at present are so hectic that we have no time in the morning except to rush to work. We are always busy, there is no time even for breakfast. While eating it in a hurry we somehow watch some TV also. We are all the while running.

That is why Swamiji recommends that we should sit quietly for some time. Some time during the day should be earmarked for this purpose and come what may, we do not cut into this time. We should realise that to lead an integrated life we cannot run away to the Himalayas and meditate. We have to face the challenges of everyday life and sitting quietly will help us to meet these challenges better.

Let us look at the stages that lead to meditation or *dhyana*. The first stage is *pratyahara*. According to Patanjali when we sit down to meditate, the mind roams about in different directions because we do not know on what we should meditate. The mind does not focus on the inner self. At this juncture we should wait and watch the mind as it jumps in different directions. This is called *pratyahara*—a stage which acts as a witness of what is happening within.

Therefore the first stage is to draw up a

routine to spend 10-15 minutes in introspection and then begin attempting meditation. As a witness we observe the mind moving in the world of the household or business or any other area of activity which engages our attention during the rest of the day. Then we are to slowly withdraw the mind from these and think that we are pure Atman, pure consciousness not limited by the mortal, material body-mind complex. As often as the mind strays from this one thought, we have to bring it back again. Repeated withdrawal of the mind from other directions and focussing it on the inner self is the process of *pratyahara*. This ultimately qualifies us for the next stage, that is, *dharana*.

The next stage is, focus the mind on any particular deity or *mantra*. The mind is to be concentrated on a particular point, a particular concept, a particular image. This concentrated focussing of the mind is *dharana*. Once we succeed in this, we are able to keep our mind fixed on a certain object at least for a few seconds to start with without letting any other thought come into the mind. This is called meditation, *dhyana*.

When this total absorption continues, we call it *samadhi*. This, of course, is out of the reach of most people and once established in *samadhi* we become *jeevan mukta*. When people tell me they meditated for an hour I have my doubts because we have to struggle hard to meditate even for a few seconds. Even to practise *pratyahara* is difficult, then we have to attempt *dharana* and finally comes *dhyana*. After all these stages comes *samadhi*.

We have to keep in mind, again, Patanjali's categorisation: he speaks of eight stages or astanga yogas before we can attempt the three stages mentioned above with regard to *dhyana*. These are *yama*—sense-control, that is to possess *ahimsa, satya, brahmacharya, astha, aparigraha, niyama*—to cultivate good habits, such as *soucha*—cleanliness, *santosh*—contentment, *tapas*—a certain amount of austerity, *shraddha*—respect for scriptures, *ponidhana*—resignation to God. Then come the *asanas* or particular postures, *pranayama*—patterns of breathing, which teaches us to inhale pure vibrations and exhale all that we think is bad in us. This helps to withdraw the mind from the world and is followed by *dharana, dhyana* and *samadhi*. At this stage one loses oneself in the object of meditation. The self, body, senses get lost in the *Ista devata* as it happened in the case of *sadhakas* such as Tukaram, Ramprasad, Mirabai and others.

Chapter 10

Effects of Meditation

When we are not in a meditative frame of mind and are under tension we are passing through a strange state of mind. In times of stress we notice that the mind is typically jumping from one thought to another. As a result of this restlessness it gets exhausted. Meditation, in contrast to this directionless activity, helps us to overcome our restlessness by keeping the mind on one object of concentration.

Meditation also helps us in other ways. As has already been noted, during the process of meditation, we can act as a *sakshi* or witness. When we sit for meditation many thoughts come to mind. Many ideas float to the surface of our consciousness but if we take up the attitude of a witness and cultivate the habit of studying all that is passing through the mind, we derive peace. We merely observe the thoughts and do not react to them. This is one of the advantages of meditation.

Those who are not in the habit of meditating react violently as soon as a thought comes into their mind. The immediate result is grief because more often than not the mind has the tendency to ruminate over negative aspects of experience. The more we indulge in negative thoughts, the more we become prone to nervous tension. But if we practise meditation and observe whatever thoughts float into our mind, we are able to see that slowly these thoughts subside on their own and the entire pattern of our psychological stress and strain begins to decline.

Therefore, it is most emphatically stated that each of us should set apart at least a few moments each day when we can dive deep into the innermost recesses of our being so that we stay free of the emotional entanglement with negative thoughts. We learn how to let go. Once we succeed in establishing this attitude no thought can produce a ripple on the calm surface of the mind. We are detached witnesses to our own thoughts and the peace this brings is diametrically opposite to mental stress.

Another important effect of meditation is

that we become aware of a peaceful state which emanates from within. Those who practise regular meditation will surely affirm that there are days on which they are at great peace with their inner self. They say that on that particular day they had deep meditation. This is one way of attaining a calm state, totally free from any kind of tension. Once we successfully achieve this state, we are armed with a tranquility that helps us to meet all the challenges that come to us during the course of the day. Amid the hectic activity of our daily routine it is good to recall the serenity of the moments of meditation which we have had earlier. When provocations come we should not surrender the peace which we acquired by the grace of the Almighty in the hours of silent meditation. We have to exercise our will-power to keep that peace constantly in mind so that the adversities of life cannot ruffle our mind.

In other words, meditation is a peaceful pause in an otherwise hectic flow of life. We certainly need such a pause. Since in our busy schedule we have not allotted any time to pause and ponder, we suffer. The corrective to this is to take the help of moments of meditation to pause and ponder which will surely have a sobering influence on our hectic daily schedule.

Since meditation serves to bring respite into our hectic lives it is not sufficient to restrict it to a few moments in the morning. Once we go to the field of practical activity during the day we may often have occasion to lose our mental balance due to the pressure of circumstances. The remedy to this was suggested by Swami Vivekananda when he said that we should also meditate while we work. The question which is often raised is: Is it possible to meditate while working? Before we can answer this question let us discuss the usual concept of meditation.

During meditation we sit in a particular posture, especailly in formal meditation. In preparation for meditation we are expected to have a wash, take a clean seat to sit on, withdraw the mind from the world outside and so on. We then close our eyes and visualise the presence of our *Ista devata* (chosen deity) in the lotus of the heart. We shut out all external activity and tell ourselves to meditate without any disturbance. All these steps constitute what we call preparation for formal meditation.

As against this is the concept of meditation in action. When we meditate with our eyes closed we may continue for half-an-hour at the most. For the rest of the time we go around with our eyes open. Since the formal type expect us to meditate with our eyes closed it is an exercise which we cannot perform for all the twenty-four hours of the day as it is impossible to keep our eyes closed all the time. During the major part of the day our eyes have to remain open. Thus the great sages have said that we should practise ceaseless meditation in order to achieve the fundamental goal of life, that is, the realisation of our true self.

We have the common concept of ceaseless *japam*, but the idea of ceaseless meditation is the priceless legacy Swami Vivekananda has given to posterity. We hear of great souls who are constantly doing *japam*. I am reminded of the Russian monk who mentions in his famous books *The Way of the Pilgrim* and *The Pilgrim Continues his Way* that in sleep, dream and waking states he found his *bija mantra* being spontaneously and incessantly repeated within.

Ceaseless *japam* is thus possible, but what about ceaseless meditation? A housewife or an executive has various duties to perform during the day, meeting a variety of people and engaging in numerous activities. Under these circumstances ceaseless meditation seems an absurd proposition.

But unless we practise the constant presence of the Lord, unless we spiritualise our day-to-day activities, we cannot achieve the objective of life. In contact with different people and various situations we may not be able to keep this continuous undercurrent in our thoughts all the time. This means that the fundamental goal of self-realisation will elude us and unless we gain this, we shall have no fulfilment in life.

Therefore, ceaseless meditation is the sine qua non of achieving the goal supreme in this life. This kind of continuous mental concentration is not possible unless we have a particular attitude of mind. With our eyes closed we see the Lord within and concentrate on Him. But as soon as we open our eyes we come out of the meditative spell and get immersed in the world. That is why it is so essential to infuse the meditative state even into the hours of our work.

The secret of practising ceaseless meditation lies in the words of Swami Vivekananda when he said, "Don't seek God, but see Him." This is a vital clue. Also, the great saint of south India, Ramana Maharshi spoke on similar lines.

Whenever anyone told him that in spite of practising meditation for long years, he/she had not been blessed with the vision of the Lord he would say, "You are having continuous vision of God. Instead of seeing X, Y, Z, why don't you see God in everyone/everything." Swami Vivekananda also said that the whole world is full of the Lord. We have to open our eyes in order to see Him.

In other words, with our eyes closed we can see God only in the inner sanctuary of our heart but when we open our eyes we see God everywhere. Then we live a life of ceaseless meditation. Once Swami Atulanandaji had said to me, "The whole life of a sadhaka or an aspirant or seeker of truth is one of continuous meditation."

Seeing God in everything is thus the meaning of ceaseless meditation. It is a very sublime ideal and may be difficult for ordinary people. They cannot practise spiritual discipline, are uninitiated and do not have the time or inclination to practise ceaseless meditation. For them the starting point is to change their attitude.

For instance, science teaches us unity of existence. Vedanta also teaches us something vital: while looking at a person we can also look into him. If we just look at the externals—body, mind, etc.—we are aware of the multiplicity with names and forms. There is another way of looking at things and that is by the penetrating eye of internal intuition. When we learn to look into things we see the all pervading Atman behind all things. Then we become established in a vision of unity. This helps us to meditate while working.

In this state we have to go beyond individual identities and be continuously conscious of the spirit behind things, that which is eternal, birthless and deathless. In other words, we have to keep in mind the truth of the saying "Chidananda Rupa Sivoham."

Once we are conscious that everything is the eternally free spirit, it would be illogical to say that such and such a person is merely the mind-body complex. If I am the Spirit, then so are you and everybody else a part of the same Spirit. In one of his famous lectures Swami Vivekananda put this idea lucidly by saying, "Worship of the spirit by the spirit." He also said that it was the duty of each soul to think of, treat and behave with others as souls.

Having this consciousness always uppermost in our minds helps us to be in the meditative frame of mind all through the day. All work becomes worship and adoration. It is not necessary to stop at formal meditation. It is, no doubt, an essential step towards ceaseless meditation but it is not an end in itself. Once we cultivate the habit of doing some solid meditation in the morning for a set period of time it needs to be supplemented with what Swami Vivekananda called as the "worship of the spirit by the spirit."

Then we are established in the ideal that everybody is Narayana to our eyes, a veritable representation of God. As Swami Vivekananda once wrote to Sister Nivedita, "My ideal indeed can be put in a few words, to preach unto mankind their divinity and how to help it manifest in every moment of life."

Acting according to the directive of Swamiji we should tell everybody that they are divine. Then our whole life gets divinised. Instead of a wrong, fragmented attitude towards the world we get a synoptic view of the world. We always breathe Brahman and every person who comes to us appears as Brahman. In this way life becomes sublime, meaningful and successful.

Chapter 11

Steps to Meditation

Earlier we have discussed some of the proven means of overcoming mental tension, meditation being foremost among them. Successful meditation we saw puts us in communion with our real self. Apparently we are all on our surface self and are not conscious of our inner divine nature. This makes us suffer from tensions of various kinds.

In this context let me cite an incident that occured in the life of Swami Sivananda, the second President of our Order. It was at the time when Mahapurush Maharaj, the name he was popularly known by, was suffering from an acute attack of asthma. He was then staying in the Belur Math. One morning a swami asked him how he was and Mahapurush Maharaj said that he had a terrible night; the blocked nose and acute asthma did not give him a moment's peace. He was suffering greatly when he thought about meditation. Immediately he got absorbed in his inner self and all pain was at an end. In that state of absorption the external world has no effect on the mind. It gave him real relief.

The secret is to dive deep into our self whenever there is unbearable agony. Then there will be no further problem. As far as rest of the physical body is concerned mother nature has provided sleep But good sleep is not a sure means of curing all kinds of tension. In sleep our overburdened mind does not get adequate rest. This can only be possible when it is trained to hold communion with its own real nature, its intrinsic self by definite methods of concentration. This is the verdict of great mystics, yogis and sages. Real rest and relaxation is possible only through a specialised technique of meditation.

Often we have the mistaken notion that a change of occupation will bring peace of mind. In times of great tension we try to put aside our strenuous work and read magazines or watch Television. This may bring temporary relief but real relaxation comes only when we learn through the process of meditation how to relieve the mind from all our so-called physical, intellectual and emotional burdens. This brings true freedom, and rest, peace, relaxation come in its wake.

It is common to pass through phases of fatigue, disappointment, disgust, depression in life. Analysed philosophically we can trace them back to psychological confusion under which we are labouring all the time. This confusion is mainly due to our inability to comprehend the actual relationship between the subject and objects of this world. As the writer, I am the subject and all what I perceive is the object. The correct attitude would be to view everything as the indivisible Atman. But instead we limit our perception to the body and the mind, or the externals. These are the categories called non-self and when we are engrossed in them we forget the real self and identify ourself with the non-self. The result is confusion caused by the limited perception of the "I".

The non-self is actually active while the real self is not doing anything. It is a mere witness. Our mistake is that we think we are doing this or that, everything depends on us; in other words we are dominated by this egocentric "I" forgetting the real "I". We are deluded by the ignorance that we are the doer and not the witness. Consciousness of the real self brings the awareness that we are Atman which is a witness, an illuminator, not limited to the activites of the mind or the body. With the help of successful meditation we become established in this attitude which brings relief, peace and tranquility.

Let me narrate my experience of dealing with the boys of a residential college in West Bengal during the period I was a Brahmachari in the Ramakrishna Order. I was having much difficulty. Fortunately for me, Swami Siddeshwaranandaji who was the head of our centre in Paris, once introduced me to one of our trustees, Swami Saswatanandaji and said whenever I had some trouble, I should seek his guidance. One day I went to him and confessed that I had an acute problem of depression. Since he was a true Vedantin and established in the distinction between "I" and "not-I" he could correctly solve my problem. He diagnosed that my problem was due to a confusion between the identity of my apparent self and my real self. I was identifying myself with "Brahmachari so and so" who had some particular duties to discharge and was facing many problems. I unburdened my situation to the Maharaj and he asked me a relevant question, "You say your mind is disturbed. Now tell me, are you the mind? Or are you the Atman?" He explained that since I was limiting myself to my mind which was *jada* and not pure consciousness I was facing problems. I should lord over my mind and assert my real nature which was the highest dimension of existence. To get rid of my suffering I had to stop identifying myself with the not-I or the mind-body complex.

We all have a body and a mind which are objects possessed by a possessor. These two aspects of ourselves have their own eccentricities. The possessor of these two is the real self. We must become conscious of the distinction between the possessor and the possessed. As a Brahmachari I had made the mistake of thinking that I am the mind. Once we recognise our mistake we can begin to correct it and here is the efficacy of meditation as it helps us to realise our real self. We find a fountain of glory within and get great peace.

Swami Shivananda once said about the meditative state, "The strain and stress of the external world could not penetrate the mind. I was absolutely tuned with my divine self." Once we reach this state we have no desire to leave the seat of meditation or indulge in secular talk. We want to continue in this divine state of intoxication and get more and more attuned to the real self. Now we get real rest in the midst of all hectic activity. We become free from all tension.

A question may be raised by beginners on the path of meditation as to how they should progress to this end. The first necessary step is to be able to sit quietly for a sufficiently long time. Then we should be able to see what passes through our mind and be willing to wrestle with wayward thoughts. Ultimately these thoughts should go away and the mind should become calm.

In modern civilization it is difficult to find even a moment to sit quietly. We have such methods of sitting quietly as reading a book or watching video. But the need is to do the same thing without any external help. Taking the help of some newspaper, or TV is not a permanent solution to our problem of restlessness.

Once we have acquired the habit of sitting quietly without any external help we should move on to the next step. For some time prior to the hour of meditation we should try to think that we are absolutely unrelated to the world and have nothing to do with it. We may have different duties as husband, wife, father or mother but we should cultivate the feeling of non-attachment to all things and all people.

In this context I would like to mention the advice given to me through a letter by Swami Shraddhanandaji, the then head of our California Vedanta Centre and disciple of Swami Shivanandaji. He wrote, "Well, each one will have his problems and anxieties, we cannot avoid them. When we have problems in our everyday life we have to solve them. At the time of meditation we should keep these problems and worries at the relative plane of existence. Remember that you are the higher self, that these problems and anxieties can never affect the Atman. When you sit for meditation, leave them behind."

This is the crux of the whole matter: even if it is for five minutes we should cultivate the habit that we are not related to this world and that there is only you and your indwelling Lord. When we try to have this feeling of being unrelated to anybody or anything in this world, we feel a sense of eternity, as if we have left the world behind and have no longer any obligations or duties whatsoever. Then when we come back to the normal plane from our deep state of meditation, we find that we can discharge our duties better in whatever role we are given such as husband, wife, father, mother, administrator and so on.

But if we forget the real "I" and get confused with all the worries and anxieties of the "non-I" neither do we get success in meditation nor are we able to control our tension in any way. Therefore, we have to approach meditation with the feeling of what is called eternity.

To achieve success in meditation it is thus necessary to feel completely detached at the time. We have to go beyond the relative phenomenal world of multiplicity. In that condition we realise that none of these relative things have actual existence and we transcend all relationships. There is no feeling of my being confined to my body or mind. God alone is real and the entire universe has vanished.

This is the only way we can come close to our true nature. The inherent powers of the mind are tremendous. Unfortunately very few people realise that they possess such a storehouse of power within them. They generally behave as if they are very weak. Unawareness of the power of the mind makes us feel that we are helpless. For instance, if a friend gives another a legacy of several lakhs of rupees which he puts in a bank without the knowledge of the beneficiary, the other friend will not be able to use the money. He will continue to think he is poor and will not be able to benefit by the legacy. Similar is the case of the person who does not know that there is power in his mind, or how to tap and train it properly. Unfortunately we manage to fritter away the great powers of the mind.

In this connection Swami Vivekananda's suggestion that we have to dehypnotise ourselves comes to mind. We are conditioned to think that we are weak and helpless that we cannot be of any use in the world. This is a negative attitude which has to be counteracted, according to Swamiji by asserting the higher dimension of our being. We have to believe that all power, all glory is within us and work hard to manifest these. Swamiji declared that we are the children of immortal bliss. It is a sin to call any man a sinner. Negative ideas hypnotise a person; with the help of positive, constructive ideas we have to dehypnotise ourselves and bring out the latent power of our mind. Therefore Swamiji was convinced that we have to constantly remind ourselves of the tremendous power within us. Of course mere intellectual knowledge about this power is not enough. It is like having a knowledge of, say, the *Bhagavad Gita*. This is insufficient unless we know how to make use of this knowledge in our everyday life. Revered Swami Ranganathanandaji often says: "Simply keeping the *Bhagavad Gita* or worshipping it with devotion will not do. One has to live it." Similar is the power of the mind. Just an awareness of it is not sufficient; we should see that with its help we benefit ourselves and society.

To manifest this inherent power of the mind we have to meditate intensely. Only a person practising certain spiritual exercises such as concentration and meditation can make the inherent powers of the mind emerge. Through such practices emotions become unified. Once the mind learns to focus on a single thing it remains quiet. For instance, a student conducting a scientific experiment in a laboratory is deeply engaged in his work. He is so wholly absorbed in the work that his other thoughts are temporarily set aside. An artist while painting a picture, temporarily forgets the outside world. Similarly when a person concentrates on God all other ideas are neutralised.

Once through the practice of meditation the latent powers of the mind are manifested, then an enduring integration of personality takes place. Such an integrated personality does not face emotional conflicts, frustrations or a sense of insecurity. The mind achieves continuous peace.

We may, of course, think that we are just ordinary people and cannot achieve all this. But we must remember that we are ordinary only so far as our mind-body complex is concerned. Behind this frail, impermanent structure is the divine spirit. This is the store-house of tremendous power. We have hypnotised ourselves into thinking that we are weak, finite and imperfect. But Swamiji advises us to hypnotise oursleves with positive thoughts, that we are divine; we are not merely *jivas*, we are *satchidananda swarupa—Chidananda rupam shivoham*. When we are established in this thought through constant meditation, the world fails to disturb the mind. The agitation caused by trivial insignificant things cannot touch the mind.

As Swami Shivanandaji said that once he was absorbed in meditation, the stress of the external world had no power to affect him. Swami Turiyanandaji used to advise us that we should live such a life which helps us to rise above all circumstances. It is not right to expect life to continue on an even tenor. Change is inevitable in the conditions of each life. When one has favourable conditions, one can easily have peace of mind. There is nothing remarkable in this state. Only in adversity if we are calm, then we are real heros.

Life is full of challenges. Meditation gives us power hidden within to face and counter such challenges. We have strength to overcome anxiety, and the real problems of life fail to weaken or destroy the stability of our mind.

Through meditation we commune with the indwelling Lord and thereby overcome mental tension. We thus achieve real fulfilment in life. Our life which holds the promise of divinity will be wasted if we allow it to be disrupted by the conflicts of existence. A disturbed mind is a matter for great regret. We must learn to control and correct it through meditation.

Once we integrate this secret into our life, we are *jeevan muktas*, liberated in this very life. There is much truth in the saying that the mind can both bind and liberate us. A mind bound by senses, uncontrolled, excitable, easily agitated causes bondage and sorrow. But a mind trained rigorously can liberate us. This is the goal of human birth which we have all received as a blessing.

Chapter 12

Meditation and its Advantages

The advantages of meditation are enduring. First of all, the longer we live in the real self the more we become aware of its perfection; then our desires and aspirations are likely to undergo a tremendous change. Old habits which contribute to mental tension disappear. Negative and harmful thought patterns dissolve.

If we forget that there is infinite strength within us we become a victim to negative thoughts. We only judge ourselves within the framework of our limitations and imperfections. We feel that it is impossible to rise above this hopeless situation. But as a result of disciplined, prolonged and regular meditation we become established in our real self and tremendous strength flows from within. We are no longer capable of negative thoughts.

The second advantage of meditation is that it gives us a clear sense of the meaning and purpose of life. We realise the transitory nature of this world and rise above the normal activities of earning money, getting married and begetting children. We realise that we shall have to leave all this behind and go away one day. There is a more enduring purpose to our existence which will come to us through meditation.

Next, through meditation we are able to establish our priorities and organise our time accordingly. Those who have achieved success in meditation know at the beginning of each day what is going to be the pattern of activities and their priority. Without meditation these activities become a mess and the resultant tension is unbearable. The constraint to do too many jobs in a limited time seems an insurmountable task and mental tension is inevitable.

As meditation becomes deeper and deeper we have the experience of the "here and now." To understand the significance of this we have to contrast it with people who are totally engrossed in the past or the future. They carry yesterday and tomorrow with them. They live on what we may call a trapeze suspended between the past that cannot be changed and the future that cannot be anticipated. It is as fruitless to think of the mistakes we made in the past as it is to worry about the events likely to happen in the future because both these can lead only to avoidable mental tension. And the cure to this malady is to live in the present. As a poet has said, "Act in the living present." What this means is to have a present-centred life. We live in the present and let us make the right use of that present which is at our disposal.

One important matter to remember is that we should proceed at a pace which is safe and comfortable for us. We are usually so busy that we have no time to pause and ponder. We want to finish many things at the same time. Meditation helps us to become introverts so that we turn our gaze within ourselves. If we are extroverts all the time we will find it difficult to get rid of tension. We have to be introverts for certain periods so that we accumulate sufficient spiritual energy within.

Thus, meditation not only helps to overcome mental tension but also contributes positively towards personal growth and gives a calm centre in the storm of our daily routine. We learn this from the life of Swami Abhayanandaji, popularly known as Bharat Maharaj who was the disciple of Holy Mother, Sri Sarada Devi. He lived up to the age of hundred and whenever our then Prime Minister Indira Gandhi needed peace and quiet she used to go to Belur Math and spend some time with him. Her mother Kamala Nehru, the wife of Jawaharlal Nehru, was an initiated disciple of Swami Shivanandaji and at her initiation Bharat Maharaj was also present. We become aware by such incidents that there is great efficacy in initiation and the ensuing spiritual disciplines enjoined after *diksha*.

In the light of this let us look at the structural type of meditation. This involves meditation with the help of a *siddha bija mantra*; it means doing *japam*. Meditation in its basic meaning is keeping the mind fixed on God. *Japam* means taking His name. If we have taken the *mantra* from a competent guru we find that the repetition of such a *mantra* produces great calmness and helps us become more mindful and balanced. As a mystic has said, unless we are successful in prayer we cannot be successful in any of our other daily activities.

On a day when we are aware that we have to do a lot of work, we should prepare in advance by doing intense meditation. This also has been validated by great mystics. The mind trained by *japam* and meditation guides us in our action. That is the reason why as a technique meditation has been considered as invaluable in overcoming mental stress and tension.

Once the technique is mastered it is effective in calming the nervous system, controlling excessive emotion, anxiety, impatience and frustration. It increases our understanding of ourselves. We find that there is great peace if we can place our mind constantly at the Lotus Feet of the Lord. We have to continuously be aware of the presence of the Lord within, full of compassion, effulgent light and the source of all our joy and peace.

In the beginning we may take to meditation as a means of overcoming mental stress but ultimately it results in positive personal transformation. As the years go by we become better human beings. Isolation, alienation are kept back and peace, contentment, inner balance take their place.

There are many people who believe that the modern life style and its activities are the root cause of all our tensions. We may join issue with them but by raising a pertinent point: it is not the modern life with all its amenities and comforts that cause tension but rather it is the attitude we take to them that is the culprit.

For instance, there is a mistaken notion that when we work for long hours we are sure to be a victim of mental tension. Working less is thus prescribed as a remedy to stress. But such an argument is incorrect. Only that activity which is motivated by a selfish, hedonistic attitude to life causes tension. When pleasure becomes the only goal of life we are bound to suffer from mental tension. Then the only way out is to cultivate the higher values of life.

This life is temporary and all its pleasures fleeting. The fundamental goal of life is to realise God. All our troubles arise because we do not make God-realisation the primary goal of our life. We give the pleasures of the world priority over this and run after material achievements. Consequently we are never able to overcome mental tension .

Once we feel drawn to inward life the practice of meditation follows as its inevitable mode. We find an interior centre of calmness which no external turbulence can disturb. All this is possible only when we admit the efficacy of higher values in life. Once we forget that God is our goal and indulge in all material pursuits, we are faced with unending conflict and strife which obscures this centre.

One more excellent advantage of meditation is that it develops humility within us. Humility is of vital importance since it eliminates the causes of conflict.

However, it needs to be stressed that meditation is different from fanciful flights of the mind. It is not meditation to indulge in wishful thinking and from such an activity we may derive little permanent benefit. The lives of great sages prove this.

Though meditation is a proven technique to overcome mental tension it has to be learnt from a comptetent spiritual teacher who has some realisation. Such teaching carries tremendous weight since it is rooted in realisation. There will be great changes in our emotional levels and the perceptible relaxation of the neuro-muscular system. As a result of taking *diksha* and practising it diligently a person will become calm and composed and will rarely get excited and angry. Success in meditation radiates peace, harmony and calm. And the spiritual vibrations of such a person will be felt by both in the family and outside.

Chapter 13

Mental Tension : Some Instances

Let us take some significant examples of mental tension. It is usual to find constant tension between couples. In this particular instance the husband would often get irritated with the wife and she gradually found it was becoming impossible to live with him. The children were growing up and the husband would lose his temper with them for no reason at all.

After a time the wife hit upon a plan. Without the knowledge of the husband she consulted a doctor. It took a lot of courage and good sense to do so. She had only one intention and that was to help her husband to get rid of tension. By doing so she would also ensure that the entire family led a happy and peaceful life.

The doctor advised her to bring her husband along one day. Casually the wife suggested to her husband that he should go for a check-up and fortunately he agreed without making a fuss. The doctor checked his blood pressure and found it normal. But he had already heard about the nature of the patient from the earlier visit of the wife. Now he initiated a discussion which he knew would surely irritate the man. Naturally the patient got furious and started arguing with the doctor. The doctor took the blood pressure again and it was very high. The doctor explained this to the husband by saying, "When you came here you were normal but in the course of our conversation you lost your temper and see its result. Every time you get angry your blood pressure rises and does immense harm to your system."

The husband got a clue from the doctor's words and became a better person. The wife was grateful to the doctor for his help and ultimately the husband was also grateful to his wife for taking him to the doctor. He realised why she had done so and the effect it had on him and the entire family.

There is another instance of a young husband who had a spiritual bent of mind. He was trying to devote some time to spiritual pursuits such as meditation and other practices. His wife would never cooperate in these matters. She was totally against her husband's spiritual inclinations. The husband could not withstand this opposition for long and gave up his spiritual exercises. He became an alcoholic and a victim to other vices. The thoughtless attitude of the wife caused a major calamity in the family. She passed through terrible agony and finally by the grace of God good sense dawned on her. She realised that her husband's sorry predicament was totally due to her thoughtlessness. She had opposed his spiritual leanings and now the result was devastating. One day she went to a holy person and begged his guidance humbly. She spoke about the ruin of her family due to her earlier attitude.

The holy man asked her to come back with her husband and instructed them to follow certain spiritual practices. Gradually there was an amazing transformation in the couple and they became valuable members of not only their own family but also of society.

These incidents underline the fact that the utility, value and efficacy of spiritual practices is tremendous. Persons inclined to inner life have huge resources of strength, light and guidance to live life peacefully and understand one another in the right way.

Let me narrate another incident, this time from the United States. There was a great scholar who taught a particular subject at a University. Once they had a seminar on that subject and many famous scholars from different places read learned Papers on the subject. This made the scholar develop an inferiority complex thinking that perhaps he was not as well versed in the subject as he had assumed earlier. He knew he was a good teacher and students appreciated him but after the seminar he began to think poorly of himself. This became an obsession till he was forced to seek the help of a psychiatrist. The psychiatrist suggested that he should recall his childhood and try to find out at which point he began to develop this inferiority complex. After much effort no solution could be found and the poor man went back to his teaching. Finally he sought the help of a spiritual person. He was taken to one of our Swamis in America. The Swami tried to offer him a solution by referring to the teaching of Swami Vivekananda that each soul is potentially divine. He tried to convince the scholar that we are not weak, that there is a divine spark in each of us. The Swami told the scholar to manifest the divinity in him, try to be conscious of the higher dimension of life and in this way get rid of the inferiority complex. The Swami gave him some spiritual practices to follow. As a result, the scholar was able to get rid of his obsession, reintegrate his personality and resume his teaching at the university in a more meaningful manner.

The occurrence of stress and stain is a common phenomenon because most people are driving themselves at a pace which is too fast. The tempo of life is such that from the time such a person gets out of bed in the morning till he goes to sleep at night he is constantly running after things. Such a hectic, high speed living will certainly destroy our mental balance and also be detrimental to our physical well-being. Our thoughts torture us. Gradually we become so maladjusted to life that it seems no longer worth living and the only remedy to this is to learn to slow down.

Let us take the example of a person who has many engagements daily. For instance, he has to go to a hotel to inaugurate a conference, then attend a lunch invitation, then some further programme and finally a dinner party. Before dinner he wants to be alone for some time but a phone call disturbs him. He wants to lock his room against visitors but in that state of nervous tension he is unable to turn the key properly. While going down in the lift he may think to himself, "Why am I a slave to so many engagements. I must slow down. Otherwise I shall kill myself. Now I will not attend the dinner party. I shall live life as a master and not as a slave." He told his hosts that he would change before dinner, took time off to be alone for some time and went down without a hurry. This made him experience amazing peace and tranquility because he had declared his independence.

Therefore, if we want to get rid of tension we have to first slow down our pace of work. A feverish hurry to do things will never give us real peace of mind. God did not intend us to go so fast. He is determined that if we move at that frantic pace we will suffer.

For instance, there was a great manufacturer who was always under tension. He would leave his house early in the morning and cautioned that he should not be given a heavy breakfast. Only those items he preferred which he could swallow quickly and rush off to work. Such people are of an abnormal type. If we keep up such a hectic pace, life is sure to be ruined. By slowing down we shall get whatever we really want. We can preserve our mental balance and tranquility by learning the art of letting go all kinds of nervous excitement.

This can be done if in the midst of our hectic schedule we stop for an interval. We have to practise serenity. In twenty-four hours if we practice serenity for even ten minutes it will do us tremendous good.

Another way of overcoming tension is to converse in peaceful terms and not shout at people. If we want someone to do a piece of work for us we can either say in a highly strung manner, "Get the work done immediately!" or we may say, "Please see that the work is done quickly." By reducing our own tension we are saving the surroundings and other people around us from the harmful effects of tension. Such an attitude is positive and leads to happiness and contentment.

When we get up in the morning we should make a resolution that we shall speak in polite, peaceful words. If we order our subordinates around it will be a very bad day. Therefore, we should learn to be silent when we feel an urge to shout. Doctors, psychologists and others say that silence is a therapy of utmost value. We should remember that it is not hard work that drains our energy but emotional upheaval or unnecessary excitement.

For instance, there was a speaker who used to be invited to different places to give lectures. He had done so for thirty years and was never tired. He always appeared calm and composed. His was an integrated personality to the core. When asked the reason for his balanced view, he said that he had complete faith in God, a sense of total surrender to Him and whenever he had a little free time he would spend it in quiet contemplation.

So, true religion does help. A genuinely religious person is one who is well organised, who has no energy leak and can handle things with more ease than a person who is unaware of the higher values of life. A person who lives a deeply religious life learns to avoid the drainage of power from within for senseless purposes. He/she accumulates so much inner power reserve that he/she can face any challenging situation without getting ruffled.

An incident from the life of Revered Madhavanandaji, one of the Presidents of our Order who had also been to San Francisco USA comes to my mind. He was a direct disciple of the Holy Mother. When I was in Belur Vidyamandir I had an opportunity to observe him closely and what impressed me most about his exceptional life is this: he was busy as the head of such a large organisation but in spite of that he led a thoroughly organised life. He would close the door of his room and devote regular hours to spiritual practice. But once there were some papers which needed his signature urgently. His assistants were hesitant to disturb him. Later when he came to know about this he said, "You should have called me. Work is also a part of my worship. Due to this delay Thakur's work has suffered."

This holy monk was punctual in everything. In the morning he would be engaged in religious practices till 6. Then he would open the window of his room and make pranams to Sri

Ramakrishna and the Ganga. He would come down after this and visit all the temples. Then he would go to his room and have a small breakfast. Next he would read the *Kathamrita* for some time. From 7 till about 12.30 p.m. or so, he would be engaged in work such as correcting proofs, attending the meeting of Trustees, etc. One day a Brahmachari came to make pranams and he gave his blessing but without interrupting the work he was doing. Nothing was allowed to come in the way of his work. In the evening also, time permitting he would be regular in his spiritual practices. In this way his whole day was so well organised that there was no energy leak anywhere.

Keeping this life as our model we can analyse our own schedule and see how much time we waste in idle gossip, or useless tasks. Most of us are thoroughly disorganised. Once we get used to following a strict routine there will be sufficient provision for recreation, relaxation, talking to members of our family, and such things. Each job should be done in its allotted time so that valuable energy is not frittered away.

We should remember that if challenges or

baffling problems come, we should keep calm and once we lead an organised life we shall be able to do so without much effort. Our brains can operate efficiently if we are not the victims of nervous tension. To develop a tension-free attitude to life we have to cultivate a philosophy of being calm whatever the provocation.

Once a patient went to a doctor and complained that he was living at such a fast pace that he was constantly suffering from tension. The doctor advised him to develop a calm philosophy of life. The patient said, "How can I do that? I cannot change my nature. I have some inherent tension." The doctor said he would give some practical hints such as sitting in a relaxed posture, exactly as the rishis of ancient times recommended *shavasana*, as if the person is dead. This relaxes the body from head to foot. Next the doctor said that the patient should also practise mental relaxation. The mind should be visualised as the surface of a lake in a storm, with many waves always in tumult. We then begin to get free of the tension by calming the thought waves so that we can make the surface placid.

The doctor also suggested that the patient

should relive beautiful scenes in memory. Visualisation of the time spent on a beach, or the Himalayas, the rising sun in Kanyakumari, a boat ride on a moonlit night are soothing to the mind. They bring peace and happiness thus removing tension. Repetition of words which have a calming effect are also helpful in overcoming tension.

Let me narrate an incident about what a person established in serenity and tranquility can do. This person was Swami Virajanandaji, one of the Presidents of our Order and disciple of Swami Vivekananda. Once a young man came to visit him among many devotees. In front of all of them he had the audacity to say, "I came to see the President, not a man reclining on an easy chair with a wrist watch and all!" We were angry at his rudeness, but Virajanandaji said calmly with a smile, "What can I do as Thakur has kept me like this!" At these words the young man was ashamed and fell prostrate at the feet of Virajanandaji begging his forgiveness. Had Virajanandaji reacted in a different manner a different situation could have resulted. But his calm and collected attitude saved the day.

We should thus learn to use such words which give us peace and tranquility. Another method is thinking about the days God came to our help. Each of us passes through some periods of difficulty in our lives. When we have little faith in Him, we can easily see how God comes to our rescue. By recalling these instances we get strength to tide over periods of doubt. We should then be grateful that we have overcome life's tribulations due to grace and in case we have further trouble, His overseeing power will protect. This will help us to keep hope alive and not give in to depression.

These are certain techniques to overcome mental tension to a great extent.

Chapter 14

Need for Regular Practice

Now we turn our attention to the situation in a developed country like America. It is pathetic that about six million tablets are used there to put people to sleep. It shows that those people have forgotten the art of relaxation. It is unfortunate that after working hard the whole day when we go to bed at night we do not have any sleep. We carry with us the conflicts of the day's activity and sleep eludes us; therefore, the only course open is to take sleeping tablets.

This particular writer I read was talking about a place called Florida in the USA. In this place machines are installed on the pavements into which a coin can be put to get an instant reading of blood pressure. When we get bad news, or are disturbed our blood pressure is bound to rise and once we know that the pressure is high the anxiety of the consequences of high blood pressure makes matters worse.

In this connection let me refer to what a great writer and thinker Carlyle said in one place: "The time has come when we should affirm the calm supremacy of the spirit over circumstances." We should ponder deeply on this apparently simple statement. When we live just on the surface of the psycho-physical level and are not in tune with our real nature or acknowledge the supremacy of the spirit we react violently to all adverse situations. When everything goes smoothly we are naturally happy but as soon as something goes wrong we get upset. We have not mastered the technique of rising above circumstances.

The great apostle of Sri Ramakrishna, Swami Turiyanandaji, in his famous book *Spiritual Treasures* has said that all of us must train our minds to rise above circumstances. When something unpleasant happens we are carried away. We have no time to pause and ponder. Most of us act on the spur of the moment. We are so impulsive by nature that we forget to be rational. As I have said earlier repeatedly, one way of overcoming tension is to acknowledge the supremacy of our higher self, to be in touch with the calm lying within our spirit. From time to time we should retire into our innermost selves and get tremendous strength which helps to get rid of nervous tension.

People who are prone to nervous tension are like vehicles in high gear heading for a collision. As against this we have to cultivate what is called the easy-does-it attitude. Although we do a hundred different things we should be able to do it in a calm manner without any kind of pressure.

Here I would like to recollect an incident concerning an industrialist I happen to know intimately. He has to attend to numerous important affairs constantly. But he always appears at his ease, does everything efficiently, never knows haste or undue excitement. I once asked him the secret of his attitude. He said, "Swamiji, there is nothing secret about it." I urged him to tell me about it for the benefit of others, if it was not too personal and he said, "Every morning we keep some time marked for ourselves; after getting up and having a wash my wife and I retire to a particular room in our house, our shrine room and one of us reads from a holy book. We recite hymns and get into an inspired mood. Then each of us does a little meditation. We go deep down into ourselves and hold communion with our real nature. This is not a long process. Once we finish, we feel energised and take up the duties of the day. Both of us have made it a point to see that we practise this fifteen minute ritual everyday. We have been following this diligently and with patience for years together. That is why we are able to lead a balanced life."

Sri Ramakrishna also said something similar as we read in the *Gospel*. Asked by a householder devotee how one can lead a balanced life and keep one's mind on God in the midst of a busy life in the world, Sri Ramakrishna said, "Well, it is possible. Since the goal of human life is spiritual awakening and realisation of God, you have to hold on to it with one hand and with the other do your duties." The world with all its pleasures is unreal. Today we are here and tomorrow we are gone. In the face of this fact of transitoriness if we want to lead a meaningful, purposeful life without being unnecessarily scared about death, we have to practise what Sri Ramakrishna advised: hold God with one hand and perform the tasks of the world with the other. Of course, he was then asked a counter question, "Sir, since you say the world is unreal why do you ask us to hold it even with one hand? If God alone is real why should we not hold his feet with both our hands?"

Sri Ramakrishna was the highest of all incarnations, the "Avatara Varishthaya" in the words of Swami Vivekananda, and he rose to this occasion in a masterly way. Smiling, he answered, "Well, what you say is true. If you can worship God with both hands, it is excellent. But if you cannot you must pay attention to the work of the world. And once you have developed genuine love for the Lord, everything in the world will appear to you as a manifestion of his lila. You will then find God in everything."

Sri Ramakrishna was asked another question about the difficulty of seeing God in personal relationships such as husband, wife, parents, children, etc. He was asked how such relationships could be spiritualised to see God in everything. He emphatically affirmed that this can be done and I feel that the way the couple about whom I spoke just now are spending some time in spiritual practices together are in a way giving concrete shape to Sri Ramakrishna's instructions.

The next question Sri Ramakrishna was often asked was whether it was possible to find two people of similar temperament in married couples. Sri Ramakrishna said that such couples were there but very rare. To be of the same temperament a couple need the grace of God. Otherwise all their time will be spent in quarrelling with each other, each will go in a different direction and there will never be any peace for either. But with the grace of God they can pursue the same spiritual path with amity and immense benefit.

Thus, before we begin the day we must spend a few minutes in spiritual practice. It will help us greatly. Whatever may be the contingency we should not allow them to cut into these few minutes. It is like charging our spiritual batteries which gives us power to carry us through the most difficult of days. The supremacy of the spirit is established by such a regular daily spiritual exercise.

The routine can be as follows: first we read a few pages of any holy book to create a proper mood. Next we do some silent meditation. Finally we pray to God for strength, peace, freedom from anxiety and grace under all trying circumstances. Without this simple routine life is uncomfortable and stressful but after practising it we will be amazed to see the tremendous transformation and benefit which it brings.

As a great mystic once said, "The day we are successful in our spiritual practices everything will go on smoothly. If we fail in it we will achieve no success in anything." Let me illustrate this with the example of Captain Rickenbacker who was a busy person and had to handle various responsibilites. These he did in a calm and easy manner. Once a friend asked him the secret of his ease and confidence in executing all tasks. On this particular day many things were going wrong in the Captain's place of work: people who were to do the work did not come on time and he was naturally feeling tense. But there was no frantic anxiety or stress visible in the Captain. He knew that being tense would not improve the situation. It was better to accept things as they came and not get flustered about things which were beyond his control. Then he told his friend, "My secret is to practise a certain technique. Everyday I have a fixed time when I wantonly collapse physically." What he meant was that he practised *savasana* of the yogic system, lying down as a dead body in complete relaxation. This the Captain practised several times a day and it gave him the inner resources to lead an admirably composed life.

The Captain continued to tell his friend, "I try to drain my mind of all tension, frustration and disappointment. Even if failure comes I try to rise above it. In this way I relax mentally. And finally I try to think spiritually, turn often to God during the day. This fills me with a sense of harmony which permits no nervous excitement or tension to plague my being."

This kind of conversing with God has been recommended by many as for instance Dr. Taylor whom the Captain referred to. In the course of his busy schedule of attending to numerous patients Dr. Taylor would lean back and say, "Oh God, I have to take care of so many patients. Please give me the strength to do my best for each of them." That prayer of a minute or two makes all the difference to a person's mental make-up.

The renowned mystic Brother Lawrence suggested a similar formula in his book *The Practice of the Presence of God*. He said that a little remembrance of God, an act of inward worship, is very acceptable to God. Amid our busy schedule we are sure to be overwhelmed by tension and to overcome this situation we send up a small prayer to be blessed with strength and serenity. As Brother Lawrence said, this gives us great joy and is the source of real relaxation of our nerves.

Once a person was asked how he handled worry or excitement. He replied, "Suppose I am in a noisy crowd amid disturbance, or a provocative situation excites me, I breathe deeply, inhaling and exhaling. I breathe in serenity, tranquility and breathe out irritation, annoyance. As I breathe in I fill my mind with calm thoughts and as I breathe out I reject negative thoughts. As a result of this I feel able to maintain my calm and go on with all the duties I have to perform.

Another person spoke about some basic rules which can help overcome mental tension. Let me put them below:

1. Don't think that the entire responsibility of the world is on your shoulders.

2. Determine to like the work given to you.

3. Plan your work and follow the plan meticulously.

4. Don't try to do everything at once.

5. Get a correct mental attitude.

6. Be efficient in whatever you do.

7. Practise to be relaxed.

All this speaks of the need for a strict self-discipline both in work and in our personal habits.

Let me tell you about our Revered Gambhiranandaji during the days he was the General Secretary of the Ramakrishna Mission. In those days his sight was impaired and he would be helped in his work by four assistant secretaries. They would read out the letters to him and he would dictate replies to one of his assistants. In this way he would complete the work everyday and go away singing a song by Ramprasad without a care in the world. Seeing him in this relaxed mood none would have guessed that he was the chief executive of the Ramakrishna Mission with such heavy responsibilites to discharge.

While working hard if we snatch moments for prayer it is as if we are taking on an unseen partner to help us in our tasks. We should learn not to accumulate work and cultivate an attitude which can be called *akarta bhava* —"not I but Thou!" We should remember that we are just instruments dependent on our unseen partner. We can depend on Him always, not only inside places of worship but in all places. God will give us the right attitude if we are able to surrender ourselves to Him.

One may fear from all this talk that to be spiritual is to be serious at all times and such a life will kill all our joy. A hearty laugh never hurts anyone. Once a small child showed me how models pose during a fashion show and I laughed for a long time. I had not enjoyed myself such a lot for many years.

Laughing at our problems and worries once a day is a good exercise. A morose expression or a grave countenance is not good because people who come into contact with such a person get pessimistic vibrations. Laughter infuses spirit and optimism into the atmosphere.

Swami Vivekananda was an advocate of this as Marie Louis Burke recounted in an incident. Once when Swamiji was indulging in loud laughter someone told him, "You are a monk, a holy man, a man of God. It is unbecoming of you to behave like this." Swamiji thundered, "What! we are the children of God! Should we look sombre and gloomy?"

Swamiji's words are significant. Let us keep them in mind. To be free from worry and fear, especially the fear of death we should laugh heartily and get as much fun out of life as possible. No tension can survive after a bout of genuine laughter.

Chapter 15

Living is Fun

The art of getting fun out of life is sure to help
reduce tension in our day-to-day existence. I
remember a recent incident of getting a phone
call from a boy who was appearing for his Final
Examination. The day before his science paper
India and Pakistan were playing a cricket match
in Bangalore. The parents of the boy obviously
were not in favour of his watching the live
telecast of the match on TV. The boy pleaded
and being a sensible person the father finally
agreed to his request. The entire family watched
India win and much tension was avoided. Had
the parents refused to allow their son to watch
the match it is possible he would have failed
miserably in the examination. By giving their
permission they gave the boy an incentive to
work harder and perform better without feeling
depressed for having missed a crucial match.

This incident illustrates how essential it is to

know how to get fun out of life. This maxim is also applicable in spiritual life. It is a mistaken notion that a spiritual person should always be gloomy with a sober countenance. Spirituality does not mean being a kill-joy because this is a crucial attitude for the process of overcoming mental tension.

At this point let me refer to one Dr. H.C. Wicks, a consultant physician at the Rachel Foster Hospital in Sydney, Australia. In her capacity as consultant physician she often had occasion to address conferences on how to get rid of nervous tension/depression. From her long experience she found out three important ways by which mental tension can be overcome. She pointed out that problems originate in our mind and nervous system. Before beginning to help patients to find remedies for tension or depression she would emphasise a universal truth: though we have a mind and a soul, we also inhabit a body which we share with the animal kingdom.

What she meant by laying this emphasis on the existence of the body is to make us aware of the changes that take place at the physical level when our mind is disturbed. There are people of a certain temperament who expect life to be smooth, always. They are unable to accept challenges or adversity.

But animals on the other hand, are better in this respect. For instance, if an animal is attacked by a hunter it tries its best to save its life by running away/escaping. Other animals which live by killing smaller animals do not brood if they are unsuccessful in catching their prey. They forget their failure immediately and try again. Suppose a deer is hurt and feels pain, it does not stop living to avoid the pain. It continues to graze peacefully in spite of the dangers around.

But human beings seem to have lost this instinct for self-healing. Suppose we are ill and are hospitalised. Instead of taking rest in hospital we waste all the time worrying about what is happening to the family in our absence. We seem to be incapable of getting rid of anxiety which even animals are capable of. That is what Dr. Wicks pointed out in her analysis.

In the course of her lectures Dr. Wicks was once asked whether religion helps in overcoming mental tension. She said, "Yes, of course, it does, if we subscribe to some religious faith and if it is genuine." Then it does help in overcoming mental tension.

Thus, the first point of Dr. Wicks's three-point formula is "acceptance." We should be able to accept what we are, to meet any situation or difficulty without losing our balance. I am reminded of some lines by the American poet, Walt Whitman. They emphasise the point that unlike animals we often over-react and do not know the technique of avoiding unnecessary anxieties. The lines of the poet are:

I think I could turn and live with animals,
They are so placid and self-contained,
They do not sweat and whine about their
condition.

This is only to underline the fact that failure is a part of living. In spite of our sincere efforts we may not always be successful. Let us accept this situation gracefully. But it should not be mere passive acceptance. We should accept with joy. Genuine acceptance teaches us how to triumph over adversity and rejoice.

In the beginning this seems impossible. Suppose a person is in great difficulty, or pain, critically ill in hospital and knows that he is going to die soon. Is it possible to accept such a situation gracefully? It is a situation which tests our power of reconciliation to the maximum and a person who cannot reconcile himself to the inevitable has to suffer from tremendous anxiety and tension.

There are, of course, innumerable inspiring instances of total graceful acceptance. Let me cite two such examples. One is of a young Brahmachari of our Order and the other is of a paralysed old lady in Digboi, Assam.

The first example of the Brahmachari comes to the mind spontaneously whenever I think of indomitable courage and the capacity for total surrender to the will of God. This young Brahmachari from the south, a very nice person was very ill and sent to our Ramakrishna Mission Seva Pratisthan for treatment. When I went to see him there I came to know that he had cancer and was about to die. He said to me with a smile, "Brother, I know I am suffering from incurable cancer but due to the grace of Sri Ramakrishna and my guru I am able to accept the fact that the body is temporary and it will go. But there is something beyond it which will survive. And that is my higher nature. Through His grace even here in the hospital I keep my mind on my own inner self which Swamiji told us is birthless and deathless." His words created an indelible impression on my mind. He was merely a Brahmachari, not even a Sanyasi yet. As he lay there in hospital I could see a divine glow on his face. After a few months he passed away and the Bulletin of Belur Math paid a fitting tribute to this exceptional Brahmachari in a sentence which said that he faced his disease with fortitude and was reconciled to his fate in a manner which was exemplary. I would like to repeat that such grace under pressure is possible only when we know how to accept an adverse situation wholeheartedly.

The second example is equally powerful and moving. It is about an old lady devotee whom I knew before coming to Delhi. In those days I was posted in Narottamnagar, in the Tirap district of Arunachal Pradesh. Every month I used to go to Digboi for a discourse at a private centre. There I invariably made it a point to visit this lady who could not attend the discourse because she was bed-ridden due to an attack of paralysis. She was the disciple of Swami Sankaranandaji, the seventh President of our Order, and everytime I asked her about her health she would say, "Maharaj, I am fine. I am all right as Thakur has kept me." Not even once did I hear a word of complaint from her, no negative expression ever passed her lips. She was all the time happy in the bliss of Thakur's grace. I knew that she could say such words only because she was able to accept her situation completely.

These support Dr. Wicks's idea about the positive attitude of acceptance and reconciliation as the first step in getting rid of tension. On first hearing the term one wonders what it means. Before we look for an explanation let me draw your attention to a similar expression in the *Gospel of Sri Ramakrishna*. In it the Master advises us to drift like a leaf, carried by the wind and this implies that we should adopt an attitude of surrender.

Dr. Wicks explains that when we go to a beach and want to dive into the sea it is useless to stand on the shore in a rigid and tense posture. Then the waves which are very high may overwhelm us. What we should do is to face the coming waves boldly in order to become an efficient surf-rider. It needs strength and courage to face the onslaught of the waves and dive in. Once we are in we should allow the body to be moved by the waves which will carry us back to the shore. All this can be achieved only if we have the right amount of self-effort, or *purushakar*.

We can again quote an example given by Sri Ramakrishna. He would often say that divine grace is like the wind. "The wind of God's grace is ever blowing but we have to hoist and unfurl the sail and the rest will be done by the wind itself." In other words, we need to cultivate an attitude of implicit faith and surrender, letting go in a spirit of detachment.

"Floating" here does not connote a kind of lazy or lethargic apathy. It is more of a positive attitude of mind. An example may help to clarify this point: suppose a person has to appear for an interview he can prepare in advance and acquit himself creditably. But if he has a rigid mind, prejudiced from before he will fare miserably.

That is why "floating" has been suggested as one of the methods for overcoming tension. But then there is the problem of applying it to non-believers because we have used words such as faith and surrender in explaining the term "floating." There are many people in this world who do not believe in God. Here we have to recall the words of Swami Vivekananda whose definition of an atheist is a person who has no faith in himself. Swamiji said that the older definition of an atheist as a person who does not believe in God has to be contemporised in this way. It stands to reason that no achievement or success is possible for a person who has no faith in himself. Self-confidence helps us to tap our latent potential and therefore Dr. Wicks's description of "floating" can be applied to all people irrespective of the fact of their belief or otherwise in the existence of God.

Another point which is crucial to our understanding of this attitude called "floating" is our awareness that people have two types of responses to a particular situation: positive and negative. Some people are prone to consider the darker aspects of life as all-important and fail to see that life has its brighter aspect too. We need not deny that life is full of dangers, trials and tribulations. But that is not all. Those who are positive in their approach to life do not spend all their time in dwelling on problems.

Many of us have seen that well-known picture which depicts two half-filled buckets of water. Near each is a person, one with a gloomy expression and the other with a bright countenance. The former says, "What use is a half-filled bucket to me?" while the latter says, "Thank God for this half-filled bucket." The former is a pessimist while the latter an optimist.

A pessimist feels dejected, morose and unwanted. He is never able to overcome mental tension while an optimist has the strength to handle any type of challenging situation.

Then we have the third point mentioned by Dr. Wicks which refers to "time." Time is a great factor which determines our life. It teaches us to have patience and perseverence. We struggle in the framework of time and also achieve success by overcoming our problems in time. Our mistakes and failures lead us to success. We must remember the words of Swami Vivekananda in this context. He said, "Never mind failures. They are quite natural. They are the beauty of life."

In this connection we can take an example given by Dr. Wicks. A young woman had to struggle hard in early life. She finally got a job and was engaged to be married. Unfortunately her father fell ill at the same time. One day when she was alone at home, a man broke into the house and attacked her. It took her many years to overcome the after-effects of this shattering experience. Finally, she consulted Dr. Wicks who advised her to cultivate the attitude of "floating." Ultimately this helped the young woman to get out of her difficulties.

Dr. Wicks's formulation is based on her long experience and similar thought patterns exist in many religious books and also verdicts of saints from diferent parts of the world. Dr. Wicks puts forward this three-point formula to help train the mind so that it is in tune with one's inner self. She believes that the patient's inner voice is his/her salvation.

My own personal experience confirms the efficacy of this advice. In 1954 when I had just joined the Order, I went up to Swami Vishuddhanandaji, the then Vice President of the Order and showed him a self-analysis chart to check how many of the twenty-six virtues mentioned in the *Bhagavad Gita* I had been able to practise. I wanted to do this as an effort towards self-improvement. Maharaj listened to my explanation and looked through the chart patiently. Then he said, "Good. But my son, it will be sufficient if you practise only one virtue." I wondered why Maharaj was telling me to practise only one when Sri Krishna had told Arjuna to follow all the twenty-six. Fortunately, I asked him to explain more fully and listened to his words with great attention. He said, "The voice of your conscience is the voice of God. It is enough if you follow this inner voice." Then he narrated a story about a child who had accompanied his mother while Maharaj was giving *diksha* on one occasion. When Maharaj asked the child, "When you do something wrong, does your mind tell you anything?" The child said at once, "Yes, Maharaj, when I do worng, my mind tells me it is wrong."

Maharaj wanted me to learn to be like the child - always open to the voice of conscience which tells us everything. Our basic divine heritage—that we are *satchidananda swarupa*—is often forgotten by us. But if we keep this in mind amid our busy schedule we can periodically retire into the inner sanctuary of our heart and hold silent communion with our real self. This will bring about our spiritual unfoldment. The inner conscience prompts us to do what is right and avoid what is wrong. We have to rise above the mind-body complex; then we shall be able to handle our tensions and lead a balanced life.

Chapter 16

Towards Perfection

By now we have established that whatever attitude we may adopt towards life we are sure to suffer from some kind of tension or excitement. It is unfortunate that tensions, worries and anxieties have become a part of daily life in the modern times. And from these conditions diseases such as cerebral thrombosis, fatigue, asthenia, obsession, depression, result. Such are the hazards of the modern civilization.

A person who is really healthy will get up in the morning fresh as a daisy with no feeling of tiredness or tension. But that is only after we have had a good night's rest and deep sleep. It is natural to feel fatigue at the end of a day of hard work which can be overcome by sleep and rest at night. Often people who suffer from fatigue all the time and are prone to tension have acute insomnia. Lack of sleep makes them tired and exhausted even in the morning.

In other words, the root of the problem is that we have forgotten the technique of relaxing. As a result, we feel oppressed, irritable, without any obvious cause. One's daily routine of work then becomes a constant effort, even disagreeable.

The charactersitics of fatigue are fluctuating moods, depression, energy loss and lack of will-power. People involved in intellectual work are especially prone to this and unless they practise mental disciplines to train the mind they will lead a miserable existence.

People who have a sedentary job sitting on a chair for long hours suffer from back-ache, headache, stiffness of the neck and tension all over the body. They should take a walk frequently to give relief to the body. Instead they brood over queer matters and become obsessed with anxiety. They find sound sleep impossible.

One very important cause of tension is the lack of concentrated attention. As the Nobel Prize Winner Alexis Carol in his valuable book *Man the Unknown* observed, "The unification of the mind to a single purpose produces a sort of inner peace." This is what is meant by concentrated attention: having only one goal at a time to the exclusion of all others.

What normally happens is that when we focus our attention on one subject it immediately shifts to another one and then another. Unless we impose some kind of discipline on the mind it will continue to jump from subject to subject in a random progression causing immense fatigue. The solution to this problem is to perform one task at a time, to concentrate on any one subject till it is complete. There are many benefits such as increase in efficiency when the mind is able to achieve with this kind of concentration.

In this connection, Aristotle's statement that "joy accompanies every perfect act" is relevant. For attaining the height of perfection — whether it is in operating a machine, cooking some delicacy or handling a complicated commercial venture—we have to work with meticulous care and total attention without any disturbance or distraction. If we fritter away our mental energy we shall never be able to achieve perfection.

Sri Aurobindo spoke about the same idea by saying that often we drift out of our inner circle and valuable energy is scattered in different directions.

Also, the example of Napoleon stands out as an instance of success due to concentration. The secret of Napoleon's greatness was that he involved his whole mind in whatever job he undertook, and he did only one job at a time. He said that when he was preparing to sleep he would close all the drawers of his mind, that is, keep all thoughts at bay, so that he would get deep, restful sleep instantly. As a result Napoleon could work even for eighteen hours each day without feeling the least fatigue.

The Nobel Prize winner Dr. Alexis Carol whom I referred to earlier said that we claim to know many things but we do not know our own self. This ignorance is at the root of our misery and tension. Swami Vivekananda had spoken about a similar matter in his reference to "Man the apparent and Man the real." We are so used to living on the surface that we are not aware of our real nature. Once more let me quote Dr. Carol who says that "Modern life finds itself opposed to the life of the spirit." As long as we limit our perception to the body-mind complex, we cannot become aware of the spirit within us which is eternally free, birthless and deathless. In this regard Dr. Carol's advice is to create an island of solitude amid the restlessness of the world. Here we find a Western thinker articulating ancient Indian ideas expressed by yogis down the ages.

Dr. Carol suggests that we should retire into ourselves and catch the music of the inner realm. This will help us to live in tune with our real self as well as achieve harmony in external life. Solitude in the inner sanctuary of our heart is the surest way of overcoming restlessness and tension.

Dr. Carol also describes how some industries create a pleasant environment for their employees to live in, with parks and other places for relaxation in order to ensure maximum efficiency at work. He also admits that it is unfortunate many people in the modern times do not care for inner life.

The fact remains that to make a significant contribution to the world or achieve something remarkable, one has to realise the efficiency of interior life and practise inwardness diligently. Great people in the fields of science, literature, or any other branch of creativity will surely admit that the source of their originality is their interior life.

A truly integrated personality with a balanced nervous system and a restful tenor of life can be achieved by retiring into solitude. Even in times of great despair our habit of solitude keeps us from admitting defeat. It gives our thoughts and actions a positive direction. For instance, a person who keeps repeating, "I am fatigued, I am tired, I am exhausted," will feel worse instead of curing his malady. Instead of brooding if he uses the same amount of energy to face his tiredness and try to overcome it, he will benefit immensely. Accepting challenges boldly in the right spirit helps to overcome half the problems in life.

Another point in this regard is to be aware of one's own limitations. Some people expect to be perfect in whatever they undertake and failure causes them unbearable tension. A more realistic attitude towards our ability and performance is therefore essential.

A few remedies for overcoming fatigue are to increase our interest in whatever work we undertake and to perform it joyfully. Often our daily duties become monotonous resulting in boredom and fatigue. This can be relieved if we make the atmosphere of our place pleasant.

Monotony can be cured by genuine love for our work. For instance, a mother who loves her child does not consider it a drudgery to look after the child constantly. A housewife works hard the whole day uncomplainingly because she loves her family and it gives her great pleasure to serve everyone.

In addition to this, if we have faith in God it is more fortunate because it helps us to think that God has placed us in a particular situation and we surrender ourselves to His will. We should also learn not to carry our problems around with us.

Apart from fatigue another common cause of tension is asthenia, a psychological term signifying loss of energy, a general weakening of activity, will-power and ability to make decisions. The most usual symptom of asthenia is a feeling of helplessness displayed by the person. A related condition called psycho-asthenia is a disease connected with fanciful imagination, conjectures far removed from actual facts. This gives rise to depression and indecisiveness. For instance, a superintendent gives notice to the hostel boarders and changes it by afternoon. The students get confused. It is therefore essential to make decisions after proper deliberation.

Brooding and lack of mental coherence are also the effects of psycho-asthenia. Another common symptom is obsessive scrupulousness.

I know of a lady who has a special *asana* for meditation and she is constantly washing it thinking it is full of germs even when such is not the case.

Anxiety of this nature is pathological and should be avoided. But there is another type of anxiety that is normal and short-lived. An incident illustrating this. The Mayavati Ashrama in the Himalayas was set up by Captain and Mrs. Sevier at the explicit desire of Swami Vivekananda. Then the Belur Math sent two new workers there—Swami Virajananda and Swami Vimalananda together with two devotees. The day they were to arrive at Mayavati it was a dark cloudy day with a severe storm raging outside. The Seviers were anxious for long hours when some luggage and two of the party arrived. Part of their anxiety was relieved but they continued to worry about those who had not yet arrived.

This is normal anxiety under exceptional circumstances. But pathological anxiety is creating adverse situations in the mind and worrying over them unnecessarily. Slowly this becomes an obsession and nerves are shattered. It leads to a variety of abnormal behaviour patterns. Will-power is shattered and the person gives way to despair.

Despair and depression have both positive and negative aspects. Let me first deal with the darker side before we proceed to the brighter side. To put it plainly depression and despair lead to the weakening of our mental vitality. A person suffering under nervous strain appears lifeless. Lethargy, lack of concentration, persistent low spirits, constant indecision are the usual symptoms. Such a person often wants to do things but does not have sustained will-power to complete the task.

A human being can be compared to a machine, for instance, a car. The smooth functioning of the car depends on its condition; as long as the component parts are in good condition it goes on efficiently. Similar is the human body which functions properly as long as all its components are fit. As soon as there is something wrong, as for instance, malfunctioning of the nervous system a stalemate is reached and various disorders make their appearance. Such a person may plan elaborately but cannot achieve any of these plans. It is difficult for him to translate even a single of his ideas into concrete action.

There is no doubt that a person suffering from depression makes many efforts to achieve something and appears very busy as a consequence. Unfortunately, the result is only a futile waste of energy. For example, a normal person can cross a busy road easily as a part of his daily routine but a person under nervous depression spends much time in thinking how to cross the road. Irrelevant thoughts plague his mind, the reason being that he does not have the ability to concentrate on one thing nor does he have the required energy to put his thoughts into action.

Depression is not evident at all times. Often instead of listlessness an agitated or excited state may appear which may also denote depression. Such a person may pretend to be full of energy and engage in numerous and diverse activity without being able to bring even one to its fitting conclusion. An unnatural surge of excessive energy followed by periods of total lack of energy are common. Nervous tension does not allow such a person to take rest. Over activity, like a swiftly playing movie is neither conducive to genuine achievement nor to peace of mind.

But there are some positive effects of despair and depression. As long as they are temporary they provide an opportunity for personal growth. One can apply to it the maxim: "Out of evil comes good." Failures and losses often cause depression and handled properly they can provide opportunity for unprecedented progress.

Once a devotee told me he was going to resign as his company neither gave him the deserved promotion nor raised his pay. He was terribly depressed. I advised him to have patience because sooner or later his situation would improve. His impulsive action of leaving the job would not do him any good. I am sure he must have reconsidered his decision and become reconciled to his lot.

Depression often helps us to build up courage or become smarter, bolder and face challenges fearlessly. The need is to treat it constructively and creatively and not make a habit of it. Self-analysis will help a victim of depression to spot his past mistakes and avoid them in future. We should take a broad view of depression so that our character, beliefs, attitudes, conditioning, behaviour and even our relationships and lifestyle change as soon as we learn to handle depression and put it in its proper perspective. We emerge from it with greater strength, courage and conviction. The secret is not to fight depression but acknowledge its existence and see how it can be used to make ourselves better. Depression can thus bring about constructive transformation in our lives.

There is the instance of the widowhood of three women and the way they handled the despair of losing their husbands. One is of a woman who is at present an MLA in Rajasthan. But when she lost her husband she was totally shattered and refused to get adjusted to his absence. In that state of despair someone directed her to me and I suggested that she should take initiation from President Maharaj at Belur Math. She was eager and I wrote a letter to arrange everything for her. This was a turning point in her life and the beginning of her remarkable achievement of becoming an MLA.

At almost the same time this lady's neighbour also lost her husband. But in the absence of spiritual succour and sustenance she found it impossible to reconcile herself to her loss.

The third example is from the time I was posted in Arunachal Pradesh. In those days I would come to Delhi periodically to receive grants from the Ministry of Social Welfare. During one such visit I stayed in Teju and was introduced to a family called Goswamis. The husband was an engineer and they had two lovely children. They invited me to breakfast and the wife, Sukrishna, served everything with devotion. Though the family had not yet taken formal initiation they were very devoted.

After finishing my work in Delhi, on my way back I was greeted with the shocking news that Mr. Goswami had suddenly died in an accident. On the Mahastami day of the Durga Puja while he was with his family a friend's vehicle broke down. Being an engineer he offered to help, although his wife tried to stop him saying it was a puja day and he should concentrate on that. He should let a mechanic take care of his friend's car. But Mr. Goswami was adamant. He went to check the car and while he was testing it, a truck hit it and in the head-on collision Mr. Goswami died instantly.

It was a terrible shock to me and I could visualise how shattered the wife and children would be. I paid them a visit and suggested they should take initiation. A thought struck me that Most Revered President Maharaj was expected in Guwahati in a day or two. But on enquiry it was found that the list of people for initiation was already complete and there was no scope for more. I decided to speak to President Maharaj personally and the whole thing was finally arranged.

These illustrate the sustaining power of faith in times of crisis. Shock and sorrow are negative emotions which lead to depression and despair. Fear of the uncertainties of the future, sudden disappearance of sources of support which we have always taken for granted and such other traumatic events lead to uncontrollable anguish. Or there might be an inexplicable feeling of guilt causing tension. From all this comes helpless anger and the mind becomes restless.

Having admitted all these possibilities of negative reactions arising from despair we should also keep in mind that it serves as the springboard for a leap into the realm of the spirit. As long as we are content we pay no attention to the matters of the spirit. For instance, the women mentioned above did not think of taking initiation in the normal course of things. But the calamity of the death of their husbands afforded them opportunity of seeking solace through *diksha*.

An instance in my own life taught me a valuable lesson: in the words of Shakespeare, "Sweet are the uses of adversity." While I was the Secretary of the Khasi Hills Ashrama and learnt to speak the local language fluently there was some strong opposition from the natives against me and the good work I was doing. The hostile forces were against our movement as it was trying to bring back the lost tradition of faith among the people of the Khasi Hills. Since I was like a speed breaker in their path they wanted to remove me. One day a time-bomb was planted in my room but they did not succeed in killing me. Earlier the authorities of the Belur Math encouraged me to continue my work undaunted and if necessary sacrifice myself for Swami Vivekananda's mission. But later they called me back and posted me in Sargachi Ashrama in West Bengal.

I was hurt and depressed. I had thought that I was doing valuable work in the Khasi Hills. Then why had the authorities transferred me from there, I wondered. But this was a temporary phase. After much self-analysis I realised that it had all been for the best. The earlier period of intense activity was followed

222 HOW TO OVERCOME MENTAL TENSION

by this phase of introspection when I had a chance to look within.

Therefore, in life no experience is sterile. There are certain areas of our lives which need attention, repair and improvement. Ultimate perfection can come to us only when we understand ourselves completely and correct the weaknesses. That is why I said earlier that we should not fight depression or avoid admitting even to ourselves that we are depressed. The secret is to face the fact of depression and work through it. Finally we will be rewarded for all our efforts.

Chapter 17

Time Factor in Relation to Tension

Among the various ways of overcoming depression which we have been considering one is to reconcile our own past and future. This can be done during the process of self-analysis and it will bring major changes in us. We must be prepared for one or more of the following changes:

1. Change in our attitude towards ourselves.
2. Change in our attitude towards others.
3. Breaking some unwanted fixed habit.

For instance, the life of affluence which Narendranath and his family were habituated to when his father was alive had to be altered suddenly after his death. They passed through a period of endless struggle. It was so acute that the futue Swami Vivekananda was reduced to subterfuge to save his mother further mental agony. We are told how he would often pretend as though he had eaten with a friend and go hungry so that his brothers and sisters got a little more to eat. It was a period of struggle in Swamiji's life which moves us to tears. But such things happen and the ensuing despair can be handled only through proper self-analysis.

This process helps us to discover the real purpose of life and provides answers to questions on fate and destiny. Once we are able to bring in these major changes in our habits and attitudes we are able to overcome much of our despair.

Rediscovering ourselves and trying to build a new life from the wreckage of the earlier one which has been causing depression and despair are effective strategies to overcome the problem of tension. With strong determination we can resolve the trouble which may at first sight seem insurmountable. Briging about effective changes is totally up to us as long as we are prepared to accept the responsibility for our behaviour, actions and attitudes. As a good General can inspire his soldiers to move forward fearlessly, fight boldly and win glorious victories against the most invincible enemies so also is an unswerving determination able to inspire an individual to achieve remarkable feats of courage in the battle of life.

Individuals can thus determine the course of their own lives if they have sufficient confidence and unshakeable faith in themselves. It is not right to just sit back and wait for fortune or luck. One should depend rather on one's own acts, thoughts, efforts, skills and values. These induce positive thought currents that we have to make our own life significant. Nothing else or no one else can do this for us. It is for us to formulate a workable strategy of meaningful existence and carry it throughout life. Then we should have no time to indulge in our predeliction for being depressed.

In our life of hectic activity where we find no time for silent contemplation, there is another aspect of tension which can be termed "chronic excessive strain." It is quite common in today's world to find people who are hyper-active. Their excessive zeal for activity is at the root of their constant and often inessential activity. The result is continuous strain, though most such individuals will never admit it.

As mentioned earlier, an awareness of our own limitations keeps us within the bounds of those tasks which we are capable of performing.

Excessive hectic activity and unmanageable responsibility makes us extremely exhausted and physical weariness is bound to have an adverse effect on our peace of mind.

Those who are prone to excessive activity are often impulsive by nature and unable to plan and execute their tasks in an orderly manner. They do not pause to look back at what is done but jump from one incomplete project to another thus creating confusion and complication which result in unnecessary tensions. Their failure to achieve any one task at a time makes them irritable.

To tackle all these subsidiaries of mental tension one needs extensive periods of discipline. It is *sadhana* in itself and cannot be perfected overnight. As already discussed, a period of meditation in the morning is the best way to begin a successful day. The calmness within us rises to the surface and keeps us at peace for the rest of the day.

Several forms of meditation are known but one has to learn the suitable mode from a competent teacher.

Let me recount my experience at the spinning factory of the Bhilwara Group in Jammu. The in-charge there, Mr. Kaul once took

me to their Human Resource Department. When
I wanted to know what was done there he told
me that before beginning the day's work all
executives gather in a place and meditate for
some time. I decided to participate in the
programme which began with music followed
by silent meditation. Each person came in
punctually, participated in this programme and
then proceeded to their various departments to
work with extra-efficiency and zeal. I was told
of the immense benefit this scheme had
provided to its participants. Many business
houses are trying similar methods today.

Of course, this method was known to ancient
oriental sages. And the western world has also
awakened to its efficacy. Once a Japanese
industrialist came to me for an interview. His
question was, "How can we have managerial
effectiveness in the Indian ethos?" With the help
of an interpreter I spoke about this subject for
forty-five minutes and the gist of my talk was
the importance of community prayer, personal
prayer, meditation, solitude, self-analysis, etc.

For an ordered existence we must
periodically observe the behaviour of our mind.
Meditation and such other processes halt the
oppressive influence of the past and future on

our mind, helping us to concentrate on the present. By getting a closer look at ourselves we eliminate those obstacles which mar our efficiency. But it is most essential to do this regularly everyday without fail.

The benefits of daily meditation are immense. In the present world it is impossible to be idle and also free of tension. Meditation and private prayer afford us time with ourselves. Strength and calm flow from within after each such session and we are better able to discharge our duties, even the most mundane ones.

Another point to remember is to do one thing at a time. If we try to do too many things simultaneously we lose our efficiency, we become tense and concentration is scattered. Each task done with our whole mind turns out perfect. Otherwise over a period of time we become nervous wrecks from constant stress.

Therefore, we should practise being calmly active and actively calm. The body should respond in an energetic and coordinated manner with all our faculties under control.

From my experience as a monk I can tell you that keeping calm under all odds is essential. As the Head of the Delhi Centre I am kept busy at all hours of day and night. My efficiency depends on the kind of meditation I have had on a particular day. Then I devote some time to planning a well-regulated schedule which goes ahead smoothly and keeps me free from anxiety and stress.

Planned activity, performed one by one will bear proper result. Impulsive, haphazard action is a sure sign of stress. This we can learn from the exceptional life of Revered Brahmanandaji, the first President of the Ramakrishna Order. After the untimely death of Swami Vivekananda everyone wondered how the infant organisation would survive. But Swamiji had put Brahmanandaji at the helm with a prediction that if necessary he could efficiently administer even a kindgom. And this proved right because Brahmanandaji during his tenure as President never made decisions on the spur of the moment. As a result his well thought out plans helped the Mission to grow and develop. The credit of putting the organisation on a secure footing goes to the excellent leadership of Brahmanandaji.

His advice given through his book *The Eternal Companion* tells us the secret. He says that even in the midst of hectic activity pause for a few minutes to gather your energies and begin again. This helps—especially people who are prone to excessive nervous energy for whom relaxation is a real problem.

Apart from meditation, watching good TV programmes, taking periodic holidays, enjoying healing music, appreciating the beauty of dawn and dusk have a soothing effect on the nerves.

In addition the virtue of *sadhana chatushtaya* needs to be cultivated to overcome mental tension. This is four-fold: *viveka, vairagya, sat-sampatti* and *mumukshatvam*, as prescribed by Adi Sankaracharya. We are concerned mainly with one of them, that is *sat-sampatti* which is an aggregate of six virtues: *sama, dama, titiksha, upapatti, shraddha* and *samadhan*. These include tranquility of mind, sense control, even-mindedness, which concretise our relationship with God, or if we don't believe in God then at least with our own self.

Chapter 18

Practising the "Presence of God"

When I was posted in Saradapith, a big educational complex adjacent to our headquarters in Belur Math, the then President of the Order, Revered Vireshwaranandaji Maharaj, visited us one day and one of the brahmacharis asked him a question: "Maharaj, we have left home with the intention of realising God. But in the Ramakrishna Mission there is much emphasis on work. Please tell us how to strike a balance between action and contemplation."

To this Vireshwaranandaji gave a very significant reply. He said, "Read the book by Brother Lawrence entitled *Practice of the Presence of God*. In it you will find that even while working in the kitchen Brother Lawrence could remember Christ. Do all work only for the love of Christ or Sri Ramakrishna. You are assuming that only meditation is a spiritual activity and all others are secular activities. But remember work is worship and adoration."

What is significant about this reply is that we can feel God's presence all the time in whatever we do. Come what may we should try to establish a sweet, inward relationship with God. Who can be a better guide to help us in our difficulties? Once we become habituated to such an attitude we cannot be a prey to mental tension for long.

Also, we should master the art of relaxation. Dr. Edmond Jacobson, the Director of the University of Chicago Laboratory for Clinical Psychology has two books on this: *Progressive Relaxation* and *You Must Relax*. According to him we suffer because we are tense and have no time or means of relaxation. If we relax we have no inclination to worry or be tense.

Relaxation is essential for everyone and everything. For instance, there is a fallacy that the heart works continuously and we die if it stops working. But the actual fact is that between contractions it has a definite period of rest and out of twenty-four hours the heart works for only nine.

With adequate rest a person can even work up to 16-17 hours a day. During the second World War, Winston Churchill did it without any feeling of fatigue because he had mastered the art of relaxing completely for the remaining hours. Another example is that of Rockefeller who worked hard to accumulate immense wealth and still lived up to the ripe old age of 90. He was in the habit of taking a short nap in his office and during that time no one was allowed to disturb him, even if it was the President of the USA.

It is a good habit to relax at least for half an hour or twenty minutes periodically. As one of the Assistant Secretaries of our Order, Revered Saswatanandaji used to say, "It will tone you up." Rest has been aptly described as "repair" by Daniel Joselyn in a book entitled *Why Be Tired*. Edison attributed his enormous energy and endurance to his ability to sleep whenever he wanted to. And Henry Ford once said, "I never stand up when I can sit down. I never sit down when I can lie down." In the rigorous training given to soldiers, a part is devoted to acquiring the habit of resting and relaxing for short periods. All these are important guidelines for curing mental tension.

It has been scientifically proved that the activities of the brain do not cause fatigue. Mental tiredness is mainly due to attitudes rather than hard work. That is to say, tension, worry, anxiety make us tired and not mental labour.

J.A.Hadfield, a distinguished psychiatrist of the UK in his famous book *The Psychology of Power* observes: "The greater part of fatigue from which we suffer is of mental origin. In fact, exhaustion of purely physical origin is rare." Another psychiatrist of the USA, Dr. A. Bril goes further and says that fatigue in sedentary workers is mainly due to psychological factors.

Therefore, the conclusion is obvious that hard work itself is seldom the cause of fatigue or nervous tension. The solution is the ability to relax. William James, in his book *The Gospel of Relaxation* writes: "The American over-tension, jerkiness, breathlessness and intensity and agony of expression are bad habits, nothing more and nothing less." James suggests that bad habits can be countered by good habits so that despair and the resulting tension is avoided. As we often teach in our meditation classes, we should breathe in purity and breathe out impurity, breathe in tranquility and breathe out tension.

Further suggestions for improving mental states are: to work as far as possible in a comfortable position, to do only as much work as we are capable of—not to overwork. From time to time we should pause to think and relax. Doing one thing at a time and completing the work on hand before we go on to something else is also advisable. The right attitude makes all the difference. If at the end we are excessively tired we should find out the reason for this. Often it is not the hard work which has made us tired but the way in which we work that is wrong. However much we do as long as we work in a relaxed way we shall never be tired.

Here we can take a lesson from the systematic manner in which the former President of our Order, Revered Gambhiranandaji used to work as has been described in an earlier context. From his example we can learn the art of efficient time management.

In the Library of Congress in Washington, some very significant words are painted in the ceiling which say: "Order is Heaven's first law."

We should bring this into our lives by being orderly in all we do. A desk littered with unanswered mail or piled high with files is enough to breed confusion and tension.

A famous psychiatrist, Dr. William Sadler tells us how his timely advice once saved a patient from nervous breakdown. The patient came to him for a remedy for his tension. But looking at the doctor's neat desk he was astonished and said, "Where do you keep all your unfinished business and unanswered mail?" Dr. Sadler said that all his business was finished regularly and all the mail was answered immediately. The patient could not believe this at first. Once he recognised the efficacy of the doctor's way of working, he managed to clear the three or four desks full of files in his own office and became more regular in his work. Later he told Dr. Sadler that his timely advice had saved his life.

The same idea is implicit in the statement of Charles Hugher, a former Chief Justice of the Supreme Court of the USA who said, "Men do not die from overwork. They die from dissipation and worry." During the course of the day we suffer tension because of dissipation of valuable energy which can be checked if we proceed in a fixed order.

Great achievements too are founded on this simple maxim as the case of the famous writer George Bernard Shaw illustrates. Shaw would have remained a cashier in the bank unless he had strictly adhered to his plan of writing five pages per day. His determination paid rich dividends.

Finally, much of our tension will decrease if we learn to delegate our work and share our responsibilities. People in power often find it very difficult to delegate their authority. One must be realistic and acknowledge that everything cannot be done single-handed. Once we choose the right people and delegate our work we shall be able to function in a balanced and efficient way.

The last word in dealing with tension is, of course, practising the presence of God and developing a sweet relationship with our indwelling divinity. Then nothing disturbs us, nothing frightens us. We should remember that all things are just passing phases of experience in life. Over-reacting to any one particular experience is neither necessary nor desirable. We should keep in mind the immortal words that even when the whole world is against us we have God on our side, always. In times of anxiety if we take a moment's respite and send up a word of prayer, it is immensely beneficial in controlling tension. In addition to this, the regular daily schedule of prayer, meditation and introspection are invaluable. A person who makes this simple routine habitual will never be a victim of nervous tension whatever the nature of constraints and challenges he/she has to face. Let more and more people accept this path and free the world of unnecessary tensions.